EARLY PRAISE FOR PATRICIA TEMPLE DAY'S *WHEN THE THIEF STRIKES*

I have been touched, moved, and impressed by this book. We have access to plenty of stories about mental illness, suicide, and grief of fictional characters and social celebrities. But how often are we welcomed into another ordinary person's life to share the full story of heartbreaking love? This book is that welcome. We check out self-help books on the subjects of mental health, grief, and loss, especially if they are written by people with name recognition. But where is the collected wisdom of the ages, the mother wisdom, that touches us with honesty and hope? It is in this book. And we look up to religious "stars" to give us spiritual coping mechanisms. But where is the down-to-earth faith that walks through dark nights of the soul? It is in this book.

—Bruce Benson, Pastor, St. Olaf College, Northfield, Minnesota

A wonderful piece of precious words that so perfectly describe the process of grieving. The author never diverts from telling the "true story" of the reality of suicide. When we keep secrets about the cause of death, we halt the process with unnecessary shame. Anyone who experiences a suicide in their family needs to read this book. [Pat Day] and [her] family have done a real service to others by speaking the truth, sharing during the funeral and with this "grief essay." We all need to know the price of mental illness. This discussion needs to continue the rest of our lives.

—Richard J. Obershaw, LICSW, Grief Center, and author of *Cry Until You Laugh*

Vivid, so vivid, you'll feel like you're sitting in the corner of Pat's home. Within the pages is a wonderful and tender picture of a world of pain—and joy in the midst of pain—many of us have not seen. This story will touch your heart and awaken a sense of God's presence in the midst of your own personal pain.

—Cheryl Horn, Christ United Methodist Church, Cannon Falls, Minnesota

A beautiful telling of a sad but redemptive story of pain and loss. As a pastor in the Cleveland, Ohio, area for over twenty-five years, I [went] often to Laurelwood, where David was treated after his first bipolar attack, where I walked with those suffering from mental illness and their families and witnessed the sense of isolation and silence around mental illness and suicide, which makes an already-difficult situation even worse.

Pat Day's story gives you the opportunity to walk in the "skin" of someone who has loved and lived through the pain of mental illness in her family. She beautifully tells the story of the birth, life, and death of her son David and recalls the ways they coped with the joys and sorrows of his disease and then the ultimate sorrow of his death by suicide.

Those who live with "the thief" of bipolar disease, as she calls it, or love those who do, will find the comfort and support that is sadly still often missing for those impacted by mental illness and suicide. Ms. Day not only gives insight, wisdom, courage, and strength for others who live with the grieving and healing process, but also helps to educate all of us on mental illness, giving a measure of meaning and redemption to her loss.

—Sally Dyck, resident bishop of Minnesota, the United Methodist Church

Experiencing one mother's joys and heartbreak when her son's life is interrupted by a mental illness provides an opportunity for all of us to better understand and help those affected by mental illnesses.

—Sue Abderholden, executive director, NAMI Minnesota

David would have been a wonderful person to know. I am a questioner and would have loved his questioning spirit. He had a good heart, and I shall remember his story and try to keep his spirit alive within me. The author bravely and candidly writes of the "blurring, numbing, overwhelming, and unbelieving experiences that we were going through moment by moment," as well as the gestures of hope and support which sustained her after his death.

—Jeannine Fraley, spiritual director/faith community nurse, Pastoral Care for Clergy and Families United Methodist Annual Conference/Twin Cities District

Pat Day tells a compelling story of tragedy and healing in this beautiful memoir of her son David's life. Anyone who has suffered a painful loss or faced the challenges of coping with the mental illness of a loved one will find hope in these pages. [Her] honesty as she recounts her own journey offers a road map to others who find themselves on a similar path after a painful loss.

—Cindy M. Gregorson, director of Congregational Development, Minnesota Conference of the United Methodist Church

When I studied psychology back in my college days, "manic-depressive" was just a label applied to people whom I might pity, be scared of, or worse, make fun of, but with whom I could not identify. How many of the people I met or who sought ministerial support in my thirty years as a priest have actually suffered from bipolar disorder, as it is referred to today, without my being aware of it . . . without my really understanding their illness and knowing how to help them?

Pat Day weaves her son David's story with her own as mother in a very well-written and moving account. She then bridges from personal storyteller to informed advocate for all affected by bipolar disorder. My ministry, particularly with those suffering from mental illness, will be enhanced by what she has written here.

—Rev. Denny Dempsey, Catholic Church of St. Dominic, Northfield, Minnesota

The phrases "mental illness" and "committed suicide" represent topics most people avoid. That is, until one or both smack you in the face. Pat Day wasn't smacked in the face—she was body-slammed on the day she learned that her adult son, David, already suffering with bipolar affective disorder, had committed suicide.

In When the Thief Strikes, *Pat Day shares* the experience of David's bipolar disorder and his eventual death. The author is not offering a scholarly text on difficult subjects. She is a mother, a devout Christian, a woman still trying to understand things that make no sense. Things like why her son chose suicide, why the God she has always trusted let this tragedy occur, why "mental illness" and "suicide" evoke such confusing responses from other people.

She offers no glib answers, no sugarcoated platitudes, no religious clichés. Instead, she shares the pain, guilt, anger, and insight of an ongoing journey. She is candid about her confusion as well as her faith. The writing is articulate, but also highly personal—Pat lets the reader see her weep and feel the darkness that nearly overwhelmed her. By sharing her journey, she seeks to educate those willing to confront subjects that remain socially taboo. She offers hope and comfort to those walking a similar path.

—Paul R. Adams, PhD, LP, clinical psychologist
and certified spiritual director, Thief River Falls, Minnesota

The thief comes only
to steal and kill and destroy;
I have come that they may have life,
and have it to the full.

John 10:10 NIV

When the Thief Strikes

Echoes of the Heart

When the Thief Strikes

Love, Loss, Pain, God

Patricia Temple Day

Library of Congress Control Number: 2010900889
ISBN: Hardcover   978-1-4500-2439-6
                   Softcover   978-1-4500-2438-9

All inquiries should be addressed to
johnandpatday@msn.com of Randolph, Minnesota.

The cover art is by Amy Canfield.
The editing is by Nancy Ashmore, Northfield, Minnesota, www.ashmoreink.com.
Foreword by Timothy Twito, MD, Psychiatrist, Allina Medical Clinic, Northfield, Minnesota
Afterword by S. Charles Schulz, MD, University of Minnesota Medical School

This book was printed in the United States of America.

To order additional copies of this book, contact:
Xlibris Corporation
1-888-795-4274
www.Xlibris.com
Orders@Xlibris.com
58271

FOREWORD

As a practicing psychiatrist for over twenty years, I still find it incongruous that the vivid suffering of those afflicted with any of the major mental illnesses is obliquely linked at best to discrete biological abnormalities whose reproducible measurement might aid diagnosis and treatment. Blood tests, radiologic scans, genotyping, and nuclear medicine procedures all fall short of being relevant to day-to-day clinical practice. We are pretty much left with interviewing patients and their families and friends and following these peoples through time, when it comes to tendering a psychiatric diagnosis, recommending a course of treatment, and evaluating its outcome.

Despite these limitations, psychiatry and psychiatrists have come a long way toward helping people with mental health disorders. Time-honored techniques such as psychotherapy offer considerable benefit and succor to patients, and medications have a half century's tradition of quelling anxiety, lifting spirits, leveling moods, and quieting psychosis. While the effectiveness of such treatments is often partial, and the course of the underlying ailments often chronic, many psychiatric patients recover sufficiently to lead full lives.

Unfortunately, stereotypes of the psychiatrically ill still abound, and proscriptions against their reentry into society in general, and the workplace in particular, remain, as Pat Day's heartfelt and evocative account of her late son David's unsuccessful effort to be admitted to the Minnesota Bar, and its tragic aftermath, his suicide, documents in painful yet loving detail.

Ms. Day describes David as being a kind of golden boy: funny and bright, curious and driven, tolerant and religious, respectful but mischievous. He's fond of school and his brothers and horses and computers. He excels in college, finds a career, and prepares to marry his longtime girlfriend when he falls ill with mania on the cusp of their wedding and is hospitalized.

We follow David through his illness's erratic course, its waxing and waning pattern hard both on him and on his family, hopes rising and falling as he worsens, recovers, and worsens again. Ms. Day is particularly good at conveying her shock and initial incomprehension at hearing her son's diagnosis, a shock soon supplanted by hopefulness that with specific diagnosis comes specific therapy, and with that relief. Sadly and not uncommonly, this optimism falters as the realities of our therapeutic limitations for bipolar disorder set in. Yet David and Ms. Day persevere, accepting that while no "cure" exists for manic depression, its excesses can be moderated and, to an extent, managed.

Religion plays a large role in Ms. Day's life, at least as evidenced by her text, both in coping with David's condition and, ultimately, in dealing with his suicide. While similarly oriented readers should find her exploration and celebration of her faith compelling and inspiring, I suspect those not religiously inclined will read with admiration for her struggle to make sense of her tremendous loss without abandoning her convictions.

Ms. Day has written a commendable book perhaps best suited for family members and friends of people struggling with a major mental illness. My strongest impression on reading it is that despite David's travails and sad ending, Ms. Day considered herself blessed to have him for a son, as David certainly was to have Ms. Day as his mother.

Timothy Twito, MD, Psychiatrist
Allina Medical Clinic, Northfield, Minnesota

DEDICATION

I dedicate this book to you who suffer the pain of mental illness and to those who love them. And to all who grieve when "the thief" steals someone or something you love.

I think often of my son David and all that his life, illness, and death have taught me. I am still learning all that I have lost and all that I have gained. It is my prayer that others who have suffered in this way will find ways to channel their grief to productive purpose and to encourage each other to never give up loving.

Thank you, David.

Your illness gave birth to my dream
That the day will come when mental illness
Will be treated with the same respect and compassion
As other life-threatening illnesses.
Your life made this book possible.
Your death made it necessary.
Though your death was the end of your life here on earth,
May your story be the beginning of your work here.[1]

CONTENTS

ACKNOWLEDGMENTS

Transforming David's story—and my own—into this book has been a long and rocky road, and I never would have made it over the boulders without the strong helping hands extended by many.

Nancy Ashmore deserves my undying gratitude for her expertise and kind and gentle mentoring during the birthing of this book. I brought her the bones of my experiences. She helped me put it together into a living story.

Krista Clark was an angel sent by God. She was a total stranger who entered my life and offered invaluable editing suggestions and inspiration during the climb. Her persistence helped me get started and moving in the right direction.

Marie Gery offered a hand-up at times when the climb got steeper. When surgeries and computer breakdowns threw more barriers on my road, her practical suggestions, like "It'll get done in God's good time," kept me moving forward.

I have had many "unanswered" prayers—at least prayers not answered according to my desires. I have learned sometimes that prayers are answered without being uttered. God knew I would need a pastor like Dan Horn of Christ United Methodist Church of Cannon Falls, Minnesota, after David's death and provided him without my asking. He listened with compassion and encouragement when I vented my pain and confusion.

Pastor Dan inspired through his life (mainly) and his preaching (secondly). His sermons never failed to give me light and hope for one more week. When he preached, I usually scribbled thoughts that his message inspired on the back of the church bulletin. When there was no room left, my husband John would hand me a small notebook that he always remembered to carry in his pocket. Some of those thoughts ended up in this book. That is, when I could find the notes. Organized I'm not. Those who think I am have me mixed up with "the other Day," John.

My sincere gratitude to my family for believing in me and for your unfailing love and support:

Son Matthew for his support, which helped me to truly believe, "We're going to get through this, Mom!"

Sons Michael and Danny, who kept the memories of David alive.

Sisters Bernie and Sharon for listening and listening with empathy, without judgment, with practical suggestions and encouragement. For checking in to ask how I was doing and giving me space to answer truthfully. For supporting me at times when I probably should have been locked in the house.

Karen Nelson and Helen and Ellie Temple, my sisters-in-law, who helped me believe that my experience could serve my passion for achieving better public understanding of and care for the mentally ill and those who love them.

Brothers Norman and Duane Temple and brothers-in-law Bert Reese, Dick Engdahl, and Noren Nelson, who faithfully supported us through the long battle with David's mental illness and death.

Sincere thanks and gratitude too to our many faithful friends, who not only laughed with us but also came alongside us in our grief journey. Each of you seemed to have God's timing when an encouraging word or deed was especially needed. You know who you are! And I believe God knows who you are! Pat Hanson (my perky but patient friend), Marilyn Otte (whose meatballs and cakes are to die for), and Mary Leean (a fine lass, even more Irish than I am!) come to mind, to name a few.

Last, but First in My Heart

Credit and gratitude to my husband, John W. Day. Four decades ago on a cold wintry day in a small white Methodist Church in Randolph, Minnesota, he pledged his vows "in sickness or health for better or worse, till death do us part." He fulfilled his promise to love and cherish me during those times and during another occasion not anticipated in our vows, my writing of this book. Delivering this story was a harder and longer labor than expected, and during it I wasn't much fun to be around.

John's faithful, steadfast love provided me with a strong shoulder to lean on during David's illness. After our son's death, he gave me the time and space to heal in my own time and way. I have also appreciated his practical contributions. He always helped me find my glasses and had a hanky available when tears came unbidden. I have needed those too.

INTRODUCTION

When I heard that my son David was dead of a gunshot wound, I initially rejected the coroner's conclusion that it had been self-inflicted. "No!" I insisted. "It must have been done by a burglar." Eventually, I came to accept the truth—that despite everything he, and we, had done, the mental illness he had battled so valiantly for eight years had finally turned out to be more than he could control. It was a bitter pill to swallow and one that tested my faith.

In a way, though, I had been right: David *had* been the victim of a "thief." Once called "manic depression" and now known as "bipolar disorder," this thief had robbed him of marriage to his college sweetheart and of his job as a computer network administrator and had threatened to steal his dream of being admitted to the Minnesota Bar and helping low-income people in a public interest law practice. This pernicious criminal also robbed his family of his cherished presence and of our dreams for the contributions he might yet make to the world.

When David was diagnosed with bipolar disorder at age twenty-five, I wanted to cry my eyes out. I read my eyes out instead, gaining a great deal of good clinical information. David's death gave birth to this book. It ripped off my rose-colored glasses and demonstrated to me the crying need for a book sharing practical, frontline experience that recounts not just the nature and symptoms of mental illness but also its devastating effects on the families of those afflicted.

I have written this book to share what I have learned on my journey but wish I had known at the beginning. To encourage a greater public understanding and acceptance of mental illness. And to offer sympathy and support to those who have suffered a painful loss, through death, accident, illness, rejection, or a dream that cannot be fulfilled. When you lose someone or something you love, you set out on a grief journey. Every step feels lonely and endless. Yet countless others have traveled this road, and limitless more will follow in your footsteps.

I share my story too to encourage those who find themselves stumbling on their spiritual journeys or losing their way and faith as a result. That path also has been traveled by many. May you discover that though life may not be fair, life and God are good. I learned more from my losses than from my accomplishments. So can you. Within our loss may be a seed from which, if it is cultivated and nourished, new growth will come.

May we find for every dream that cannot be realized, another which, though different, will fulfill our heart's desire.

Joy and sorrow are inseparable . . . together they come, and when one sits alone with you . . . remember that the other is asleep upon your bed.

—Kahlil Gibran

CHAPTER 1

No, No, No!

Tuesday, April 19, 2005

Is there no balm in Gilead? Is there no physician there?
—Jeremiah 8:22 KJV

Sometimes we want to turn back time, start over, and rewrite the script.

April 19, 2005, was a good day to be alive, a beautiful spring day. Driving back to our farm home, I mused over my morning. My husband John, my best friend, had sent me off early with a smile and a kiss. Our four sons, now in their twenties and thirties, cherished their memories of growing up on our family farm; but Mike, Matt, David, and Danny had each chosen other careers. John and I looked forward to phone calls and visits short and long. What more could we ask? Maybe a grandchild or two someday, but there was no hurry on this.

On my way to an Islam class offered by the Cannon Valley Elder Collegium in Northfield, I dropped off some information for my high school class reunion at a classmate's home. We didn't have time to chat long, but we looked forward to the celebration.

After class, I met a friend for lunch. Both mothers, we exchanged joys and concerns about our children. My main concern was David's bipolar disorder and how it affected the life of each of us in our family. Sharing my worry felt good. Our conversation ended on a positive note. David, thirty-three, was doing well these past three years after finding a medication with fewer side effects. With his intelligence and spirit, he would be a compassionate lawyer and advocate for people suffering from this horrible disease.

After our third cup of coffee, we walked together to my car. On the short trip to her home, we chatted a bit about the beautiful day. New life and color was everywhere: tulips, daffodils, and leaves popping green against a deep blue sky with billowy white clouds. We expressed our joy of experiencing spring after the starkness of winter. A quick hug and I was on my way home feeling relieved and peaceful, looking forward to reporting to John the details of a busy morning.

My ordinary, happy day ended when I steered the car into our driveway and saw John's face through the large glass window of our family room. He looked worried. *It's probably just my imagination*, my inner voice assured me. *He is just deep in thought.* I quickly gathered my things from the backseat and closed the car door.

John met me at the door to our family room and said, "Pat, come in quickly. I have something I need to tell you." My imagination raced like a thoroughbred running to the finish line. *God forbid, has one of our kids been in a car accident?* I wondered. I rushed inside, my heart pumping. I needed to get whatever this was over with now.

John closed the door, which had been left open to let in the spring air. Closing it softened the noise of cars, trailers, delivery trucks, and birds chirping blithely high in the trees. Through the windows I could see daffodils waving in the breeze. Instead of his usual hello kiss, John walked with me to the davenport, waved his arm, and said, "You need to sit down."

As I sat down, John began to pace back and forth, head down. I could see he was fighting back tears. He looked up and said, "I have bad news. David injured himself."

My heart stopped. Suddenly too fragile to move even my hands, I stared at John and asked, "How bad?"

John took a deep breath and moved slowly toward me. "He's dead."

"NO!!!" I screamed, denying, rejecting, not wanting to believe, refusing to believe.

I sat like a statue.

Locked in grief and unbelief, John and I sat close together on the davenport. I looked out the windows and saw the daffodils waving in the breeze. Inside, I was a block of ice-cold granite.

There were no words. John and I held each other in silence. Silence, loud silence, and pain too deep for words. But words were necessary.

Our conversation is forever burned in my mind, though words, when we found them, were choppy as whitecaps on a cold lake during a storm.

ME: What happened?

JOHN: Self-inflicted.

ME: NO!!!! [*screaming*]

ME: How?

JOHN: He shot himself.

ME: When?

John turned toward me and held my hands tightly. He began, "Let me explain. I was concerned when David did not return my calls. After leaving several messages these last two days, I called again this morning. A woman's voice answered his phone and asked who I was. I told her I was David's father. She then gave the phone to a man, the coroner. He told me David was dead and that he believes he died four or five days ago."

John added that a friend of David's had left a message on our answering machine too concerned because David had not returned his calls. John said during the last few days he also had made several calls to David's apartment and left messages to call him back, but David had not returned his calls either.

My mind screamed, *No, no, no! Not possible! Not David. Not our David. Not our life-loving, life-affirming, kind, generous, humorous, talented, smart son. He has so much to give, too much to live for!*

John couldn't hear my silent scream, but he felt it. Quietly, he told me that the coroner seemed kind and caring. Kind and caring, important always. Absolutely necessary for us now in our time of deepest need.

"I do NOT believe this," I said. "He was murdered. You remember about a year ago? A thief broke into his apartment at 2:00 a.m. The noise woke David. He walked up to the man and asked, "What the hell are you doing here?" The man turned and ran away. David called the police, and he was captured. I bet some thug broke in and killed him."

"The coroner said the position of the bullet strongly suggests it was self-inflicted," John responded. "He handled it in a gentle way, but he didn't think there was much doubt that it was self-inflicted."

I insisted, "I still think he was murdered."

I did not ask the big question: *why?* Not then. But I would ask and ponder this question many times during the days and years that followed. Who knows the mind and pain of another person? Who would want to? I would learn some mysteries are not meant to be solved.

John and I sat together, trying to hold each other up. Sometimes knowing the details can explain death. Can comfort. There was no explanation. There were no words, no words. And certainly no comfort.

I looked through the family room window. Why was the traffic still rushing by and the sun still shining? Why were the birds still singing and the daffodils still waving? Outside, life was going on its way. Mine was changed. It was gray and lifeless.

During the next hours I was able to function, but I did not think. Acceptance, painful as it would be, was a long way away.

Only twelve days ago David had stopped in briefly at the house, I remembered. I invited him to lunch, but he said he had things to do. His mood was friendly, upbeat, and focused. After a brief chat and a big hug, he was on his way in his red Toyota. David liked that car, and so did I. Snappy, perky, and colorful, it was a lot like David.

Why didn't I *insist* he stay a while? Little did I know it was the last time I would see him.

Calls for Help

John and I clung to each other. Our first thoughts were of David's three brothers. Those calls were too hard to make right now. Telling Mike, Matt, and Daniel that David, their loyal friend, the brother each could always count on in a pinch, was dead? Impossible.

Our human instincts kicked in before all the reality hit home. What we needed now, we decided, was the support of longtime close friends. We needed to know at least that they were on their way to our side. Maybe then we could make the calls to David's brothers. Six difficult phone calls were made: to my two sisters and two brothers and their spouses, Bernie and Bert Reese, Sharon and Dick Engdahl, Norman and Helen Temple, and Duane and Ellie Temple, and to Karen and Noren Nelson, John's sister and her husband, and to Pastor Dan Horn.

Their voices were lifelines. They clung to us. We clung to them.

Bernie and Bert were home when I called. "I have bad news. David is dead. He shot himself." They came immediately.

John called Norman and Helen, "I have bad news. David is dead. He shot himself." They came immediately.

Each time we gave the shocking news made it more and more true.

Sharon and Dick Engdahl and Duane and Ellie Temple were not home. We left messages on each answering machine asking them to call us as soon as possible. Later that evening both couples returned our call. When they heard the tragic news, they wanted to come at once. I told them, "We are exhausted. Please wait and come tomorrow morning. We will need you then." They did.

Duane and Ellie were still coping with their own loss, the murder of their son-in-law's brother and his wife. Among my first words to them were, "I'm thinking a mistake was made. I think David was murdered. I'm hoping it was murder, not suicide." Either way I would not see David again. Either way I would have no way to say goodbye. They wanted to come immediately, but I urged them to come the next morning. They did.

John called Karen and Noren in Florida. We could not see them, but tears and words of comfort and love came through the lines across the states as they shared our sorrow.

For each of these calls, the horrified response was the same: "NO!"

"No." It's often the first word a child speaks, the first word we learn. *No* means denial. It means "I can't cope because I didn't want to hear it." It means "I can't believe it, I won't believe it."

Bernie and Bert and Norman and Helen brought food, comfort, words, hugs, normalcy. It was good to see them, but they couldn't fill the black hole in my heart. I wanted David back.

Pastor Dan came soon after them. When he walked in the door, John's first words were, "I love David. But I am *so angry* with him. I'd like to kick his butt."

I said, "I could never be angry with David. *I am angry at God!*" I don't recall saying this, but Bernie assures me that I did—and reminds me that I added immediately after that, "*But I love Him.*"

Truly, I felt no anger toward David when I learned of his death. Or during the three days before the funeral. Nor in the following years. I couldn't find any anger then and haven't been able to since. Instead I felt sad and helpless. I remembered eighteen happy years of raising him. I was thankful for those years but sad for the dreams I had for his life, dreams that were now ended.

*   *   *

Now we made the hardest calls. David's three brothers loved him and always will. We had no words to soften the blow. We told Mike, Matt, and Daniel their brother was dead, accompanying the news always with "I love you."

John called Mike and, since he was not home, left a message for him to call us immediately.

He then called Matt at work, giving him the terrible news. Matt said he would be home immediately. "*Please* drive carefully," John pleaded. Coworkers urged Matt to let them drive him, but Matt was adamant he needed to get home immediately and would drive himself. I worried about him driving in traffic. Could he do that safely after such a shock? How wonderful it was to see him as he came through the door, fighting his own sadness to give us encouragement.

Danny and his wife Kasumi had been in Heidelberg, Germany, only two days when they received the shocking news. Not even enough time to recover from jet lag.

Only a month earlier we had had such a wonderful week with Danny and Kasumi. Danny had just been hired to produce the local newscast aired on the American Armed Forces Network television station in Heidelberg. We had had so much fun visiting and eating together—despite the huge amounts of time Danny was having to spend doing handfuls of paperwork to fulfill army requirements for his application. David's technical knowledge had been a *big* help in completing and forwarding the documents and keeping the process going.

Danny got the news at his new job in Germany and then drove home to cry and be comforted by Kasumi. He immediately booked the first flight available so they could be home the next day. Even in my anger and grief, I thanked God for giving mankind the intelligence to make the fast airplanes, which made it possible for our whole family to be together to share our sorrow and memories.

As we waited for Danny and Kasumi to return, Matt provided a strong shoulder to lean on. His first words when he walked in the door with tears in his eyes were, "We're going to get through this, Mom." Not you, not I, *we.* He then offered some practical suggestions. First was that he and I should take a short walk on our field road. He knew me. He knew I had to keep moving.

Mike lives close by and often drops in without calling. Since he had not yet heard the shocking news of David's death, when he saw cars in our driveway, he assumed we had company. He walked in the door, and we collapsed in each other's arms. More hugs and tears! He lightened the sorrow by sharing happy and poignant memories of David.

Norman went to buy food. Helen and Bernie laid out cold meats, chicken, potato salad, and coleslaw. I sat on the couch. "I don't want food. I want someone to cry with me." They both did.

Later I put some food on my plate, only to dump it in the garbage can later when no one was looking. I repeated this several times. Ingrained in my mind was the old saying "If you don't eat, you will get sick." I didn't want to get sick, but I just couldn't eat.

The grieving had not yet begun. Our hearts were not ready to accept what our minds understood. This process would take much time, more time than we realized.

I felt God had let me down. Hadn't God heard when I told Him I could not handle suicide? I knew the statistics for bipolar disorder and suicide. A friend had looked it up and told me that chances were fifty-fifty in severe cases like David's. But statistics are only statistics. I knew that if anyone could beat this, David could.

That night I stood in my nightgown and looked at my sad face in the mirror. So often I had felt deep sympathy and agony for people who had to endure what I was now facing. What would happen to me? Would I ever laugh again? I took two sleeping pills and went to bed. Sleep eluded me.

My mind raced. Could there be a mistake? David dead? I would have to live the rest of my life without him? So would John, Mike, Matt, and Danny. How could we? Who would lift our spirits with his wit and determined spirit? Who would keep us up-to-date on world events, technology, movies?

My sorrow turned to anger. Will people ever understand mental illness? Will it ever be treated with the respect and seriousness it deserves? Why isn't more research being done for better medications? When will this happen, Lord? When will we understand?

As a lay speaker for our church, I occasionally give the sermon when our pastor is on vacation. Once I had shared with the congregation how mental illness is as life changing, life shortening, and life threatening as heart disease and other major illnesses. Could I have foreseen and prevented David's death? Was I to blame for not doing more?

After five or six hours, I finally went to sleep. I never got the answer to these questions. I'm still asking them. My dream since David's first bipolar attack had been that he would be an advocate for those suffering from the horrible disease he had and for other mental illnesses. His voice had been silenced. And not just there, I realized with pain.

I would never hear his voice again. During the coming days I would dial his number several times hoping to hear his phone message. It had been removed. I could not even hear his voice on a recording. His voice was silenced there too.

I thought of the time several weeks earlier when David had called and sounded sad. "Mom, pray for me." I told him I would immediately call Pastor Dan. Pastor Dan and I prayed together on the phone. We prayed for David, who had so many questions regarding faith. In our prayer, Dan gave David to God. Did I call David back? I think so, but I can't remember our conversation. My memory is fuzzy at this point. I had no idea that this would be one of my last talks with him.

Last times. My mind drifted again to the day when David had stopped by to say hello. I suggested we go out for lunch or he come in to visit, but he said he was in a hurry. He, like me, was often in a hurry. Our visit, though cheery, was short. That was the last time I saw him.

Wednesday, April 20

I got out of bed. I looked in the mirror as I brushed my teeth. Who was that old woman in the mirror? Would she ever be happy again?

I felt that a dam had burst inside of my mind. I paced the floor. Then I went outside and walked our field road. Unwelcome thoughts popped in my head. The next time I filled out a medical report, I would have to put a check beside "Any suicide in your family?" So would the rest of my family. Hadn't I often told close friends, "I guess I can take anything but suicide"?

The habits of living continued.

Wednesday brought relief. Danny and Kasumi arrived home from their twelve-hour flight. My eyes filled with tears—joy to have them home and sadness for their pain. More hugs. Why don't doctors prescribe hugs along with medicine? Hugs are comforting. I still could not sit still, so Matt suggested we go for yet another walk on our field road. When we returned, our yard was filled with cars from visitors and people bringing food.

News travels fast in a small town. The pastor said the phone rang off the hook at the parsonage of our church the first day. Our friends wanted to know about our tragedy and were eager to help. Pastor Dan told his wife Cheryl to advise them to give us a "family day" before coming to the house. You don't know how good people are until a tragedy hits home. I would rather have learned this an easier way.

Our many visitors brought sanity and grace to our home. There was food on the counter, food on the kitchen table, food in the refrigerator, more food put in the freezer for later. Helen was right: we might not want food, but we needed it.

Friends hugged. In their embraces I could feel their desire to take some of the pain off our shoulders. Some cried, some offered words of comfort, some struggled for words but found none. In all cases, love shone through their eyes. My faith that people are good was renewed. I was thankful for each person in the house. Still, as good as people were, there were times I was overwhelmed and had to retreat to my bedroom to be alone.

Our friends took my mind off the next day and the saddest job John and I have ever done: planning a funeral and burying a son. Nothing in life prepares you for this. The death of parents, while sad at the time, is not the same as this blurring, numbing, overwhelming, and unbelieving experience. We were taking things moment by moment. Our hearts had not yet accepted it, but our minds knew that somehow a funeral must be planned.

Because of the state of David's body, one decision was made for us: cremation, not embalming. John said that strangely the same morning we got the news of David's death, he and his friends at the Randolph Agra Center had been discussing the advantages of embalming and cremation. Most had preferred cremation.

The funeral was set for Saturday. We wanted Danny and Kasumi to have an extra day to recover from jet lag from their long flight home, especially since they hadn't been in Germany long enough to recover from their long trip two days before from Minneapolis to Heidelberg.

Thursday, April 21

There were more visitors and more food. There must have been a mastermind planning all the food that appeared at our house. There was such variety and everything we could possibly need—fresh breads, cold meats, hot dishes, salads, pop, fruit juice, all paper and plastic products for eating, coffee, flowers. The daily cards, hugs, and comforting words upheld us.

John, Matt, Mike, Danny, and Kasumi grazed—sometimes standing in front of friends, sometimes at the picnic table or the davenport. I was still unable to eat. I remember thinking how nice it was to see all these people, many of them friends I had not seen for a year. But always the same thought zoomed in my mind. *I would much rather have David back than see them all.*

In some ways Thursday was the hardest day. John, Pastor Dan, Matt, and I went to the mortuary to arrange the funeral and choose an urn. The details of the funeral seemed unimportant. I wanted David back.

In my adult life I have always looked to scripture to give me comfort and guidance and answers to questions and doubts. I had no idea what to pick for the service. My mind was in a whirl, trying desperately to focus on what we were doing. I wanted David back.

When asked for our preferences regarding hymns, scripture, and other matters, I blankly said whatever first came to mind. I wanted to be strong for John, but my mind was not cooperating. I wanted David back.

God had the right man in the right place. We desperately needed Pastor Dan's compassion and wisdom. The memory of our last prayer for David flashed in my mind. Tears unbidden flowed suddenly from my eyes. I sobbed. "This is *not* what I meant when we prayed and gave David to God." Pastor Dan assured me that God understood our feelings. His comforting words are stored in my memory along with my tears. He was a gentle and strong shoulder to lean on. Still I wondered, would my hurting heart ever heal?

I was never so glad to leave a building in my life. We could not wait to get home. Our kids and most of my family were waiting there. My sister Sharon said her daughters Katy and Jessica were coming later that night. She hinted there would be a surprise. "Nothing bad, I hope," I blurted. "No, something you will like," Sharon assured me.

We hastily put some of the food that had been brought on the dining room table, crowded extra chairs around it, and shared a wonderful feast. Marilyn Otte's rocket meatballs and mashed potatoes, along with the other dishes, were delicious!

Midway through the meal, my nieces arrived with a cooler full of soft drinks, more food, and more paper products.

Then the men left, and the mystery gift was brought outside to our yard.

What a wonderful surprise! It was a beautiful granite bench for our lawn for a memorial of David. There were symbols of the four seasons—a snowflake, a tulip, sunflowers, and a fall leaf. We chose to put the bench under a tree on our front lawn. I sat on it and somehow felt the nearness of David.

A bench for all seasons for our son of all our seasons, I mused as I sat there. John nailed a plaque on a nearby tree with the inscription "In loving memory of David, 1971-2005."

Later in the evening, David's brothers and cousins looked through a few of our thirty-five family photo albums and chose some of the photos for a display at the visitation. Priceless memories of David and our family were within those covers. Every time we remembered another funny thing David had said and done, we laughed until our sides hurt and tears rolled down our faces. Later Matt asked me if it was wrong to laugh that much so soon after David's death.

Every day for several weeks after walking our field roads, I spent some time sitting on David's bench feeling the warmth of my family and memories of David.

Friday, April 22

On Friday a neighbor came to arrange food in the refrigerator and freezer and do a little vacuuming. I had been doing my best to record names of people who brought food and other items. John, ever the organizer, labeled two notebooks to keep records intact. Many unexpected kindnesses are recorded in those pages.

I decided to get my hair done before the visitation. As soon as I sat down, I told the beautician the hard, cold facts. "If I act a little spacey, it's because I am dazed. Tomorrow is the funeral for my son, who committed suicide." She seemed knowledgeable about bipolar, so there was no need to explain the illness, symptoms, and possible consequences.

During my hair job, we both cried, but the hairstylist cried more. I told her tears were a gift. I wished they came more easily to me.

Strangely there was a picture on the wall of a young man who looked a lot like David. Dark piercing eyes that seemed to look right through you, dark hair, so handsome. About a year later the picture was replaced. I missed the picture a lot.

*   *   *

The hardest part of the visitation was walking into the room. I could not see David; I had not said goodbye. For the first time in my life I knew what it meant to be in the black hole of oblivion. I felt all alone in a room beginning to fill up with people. I walked by myself over to David's urn and knelt before it. I cuddled it with my hands and pressed my lips to it. "I love you, David."

I had often empathized with survivors of 9/11 but never so closely. Having no time to say goodbye to one you love deepens the pain. I prayed that God would send his angels to say goodbye to him for me.

Our pastor had a short devotion before the official time of visitation. I have no idea what he said, but I know how I felt. Comforted in my heart. He brought the presence of Christ.

God chose the right person to be the first to go through the visitation line. She talked frankly about having no idea what I was going through. She said anytime I wanted to talk, cry, swear, or scream, to give her a call. How did she know how much I wanted to scream?

The faces are blurred; but I remember hugs, tears, laughter, and looking down a long line of familiar faces waiting for more of the same. For three hours people came. Nearly all said something that comforted my heart. I began to believe I was not alone in my grief. They brought the presence of God's love. Peace and comfort, they say, is not the absence of pain but the presence of love. Is that our preview of heaven, to see and feel God's love in people's faces and words? I shook hands, hugged, and kissed. And I heard again and again stories of family members or friends who also had suffered from mental illness some even resulting in suicide. Lifetime friends sharing this ache in their heart with me for the first time, letting the ghost of another person with mental illness out of the closet. Ghosts that never belonged in the closet in the first place.

Later, pondering this, I realized that people are hesitant to say the S-word with people who they think do not have understanding. They need to, though. Like all diseases, mental illness will not go away by not talking about it. It is here to stay. It needs to be dealt with.

Our whole family was sustained by the support we felt that day. We needed each other. I remember with tears in my eyes how my brother Duane and sister Bernie constantly brought me water during the visitation. What is needed more than a cup of cold water given in love? Jesus said whoever gives another a cup of water is giving it unto Him.

Saturday, April 23

> The Eternal God is your Refuge,
> and underneath are the everlasting arms.
> —Deuteronomy 33:27 NIV

The day of David's funeral is carved forever in my heart. I remember colors: blue sky, black funeral clothes. I remember eyes turned down, bodies crowded in the waiting room, my throat so tight I could hardly breathe.

It was a horrible yet important day. Why don't I remember each and every detail? I was in a daze, unbelieving, sad. I was in a black pit with no light and no way out.

I walked in the door. My legs moved, but I felt detached from my body. Where was I? What was I supposed to do now? I was like an actor in a play who has never read the script. I wanted to run away, but there was no way out. I saw people talking, carrying in chairs, preparing food, as if everything was normal. But nothing was normal. Nothing would ever be the same. For me, for John, for Mike, Matt, Danny, and Kasumi. Most of all, for David, whom we loved so much. We did not yet know the extent of our loss. That would take time, much time.

Faces blurred. I walked by the kitchen, which was crowded with our devoted United Methodist Women, other church members, and many friends working to prepare a delicious dinner. Walkers made a clicking sound on the floor as the older members maneuvered in and out to do their tasks. Funerals show respect and love for a beloved fallen brother. They also provide opportunity for conversation and community spirit. Today it was silent. The usual chatter and laughter were gone.

The next necessary stop was the restroom. One person was there, the right person. Francis hugged and consoled me. "Everyone in the kitchen is so sad. You're in our hearts." I nodded and walked away to join my family, but turned back as soon as I went through the door. I had forgotten to wash my hands.

Our extended family was squeezed together in the room adjoining the sanctuary.

I'm not sure the number of people. There was John's stepmother, Grace. My brothers and their families. My sisters and their families. Counting nieces, nephews, grandnieces, and grandnephews, there must have been fifty-one people, I guess. Their eyes were down. I felt dazed, almost dizzy. I was too sad to cry. I grabbed the wall to hold myself up. John reached out his arm to embrace me, so steadying and soothing. Pastor Dan and the ushers entered to get more chairs for the funeral. The church was packed. Some had to stand in the back of the church.

Pastor Dan joined us. His voice forced my mind to focus on what was happening. "I've got to be honest with you. This is going to be a tough one." John put his arm around me when he prayed. At least that seemed normal.

We entered the church and sat down. My body was numb. I wanted this to end quickly, yet I wanted it to never end. It would end, and we would return home. A home without David. A home where he would never be seen again. A house without his terrific laugh. Rooms empty of his smiling deep blue eyes. No smell of his aftershave, the feel of his rough face (even when freshly shaved) when he hugged me. Rooms cold without his humor and wit to challenge our minds and our hearts.

Some memories are soothing. The packed church and kind faces. Gentle, caring words. Sad eyes looking into ours.

Rays of light entered with the service. The music soothed our aching hearts. Linda and Jim Kvanbeck and Beth Hagermeister sang "In the Garden." Our souls were lifted.

Pastor Dan did a wonderful job of capturing David's spirit and personality when he delivered the funeral message. He had enjoyed David and grasped who he was, an outgoing person who readily accepted and loved people. David had had several good talks with Pastor Dan, who has a God-given talent of seeing the soul of another person. David was curious by nature, always asking the "hard" questions. He was nurtured in the Christian faith and accepted it easily as a young person. After college and career, doubts surfaced. This is natural for all of us. I feel the example of the disciples shows doubts can coexist with faith. Is not some doubt healthy?

I believed with all my heart that Christ died to pay for the sins of *all* people and all who accept His gift and believe will live forever with Him in the wonderful place He has prepared. Now my own beloved son had died. I believed he had lived a moral life. Yet I had also heard his doubts. I was in turmoil.

A verse that comforted me was one that Pastor Dan used at the funeral from Matthew 28:16-17. "Then the 11 disciples went to Galilee, to the mountain where Jesus had told them to go. When they saw him, they worshiped him; but some doubted." These same eleven disciples were commissioned in the next verse with the Great Commission. Surely this indicates God has a plan for both believers and doubters. All people struggle with their doubts and their faith. We are all on this journey together. A wise man said, "Answers divide us, questions unite us." Doubts can lead to a deeper faith. Pastor Dan assured me that he believed David was a searching believer. He believed David was in heaven. God knows everyone's hearts, he said. God had heard my prayers.

> I tell you the truth, you will weep and mourn while the world
> rejoices; you will grieve, but your grief will turn to joy . . . .
> Now is your time of grief, but I will see you again, and you will
> rejoice, and no one will take away your joy.
> —John 16:20, 22 NIV

The service was a wonderful tribute to David, what he stood for, his questioning mind, his resilient spirit in the trials of his illness, his humor. Though his tragic ending compounded our grief, nothing could take that away from us. I who knew him so well longed to stand and pay tribute, but I knew it was more than I could bear.

Many there were asking and would continue to ask, "Why?" As Pastor Dan shared his personal memories of David, memories of a caring, bright, challenging young man who stretched him, his message was perfect: "Why it's OK to question." David would have liked it. How I wished he could hear it too. I prayed the words would enter our hearts and remain forever. I believe my prayer was answered. The long, hard work of grieving lay ahead, but these words (see following page) helped.

Doubts can lead to a deeper faith.

Why It's OK to Question! David's Gift to Us
A Reminder to Ask, Why?

Pastor Dan Horn
Christ United Methodist Church of
Cannon Falls, Minnesota

When I remember David, I immediately think of the question, why? Because that was a key word in our relationship with each other.

On every occasion that we spent together, David inundated our time together with wonderment . . . a sense of question, wondering, why?

Why did God allow . . . ???

What do you think about . . . ???

What if . . . ???

Our last time together [April 7 for lunch] was spent talking about the Terri Schiavo situation and what was best. And why.

David wrestled with questions of why. He struggled with life's difficult questions and was willing to admit it.

I love this picture of David reading a book . . . Pat said David spent a lot of time reading. This past week while in his apartment, I looked at the books on his bookshelves and the books he had checked out from the library . . . it was clear that David was seeking and looking to find understanding.

This picture will remain in my mind as I remember the *legacy* of David.

We can learn. We must learn from David. It's OK to question. In fact, it's important for us to question, to wonder why, to wrestle with life.

Too often it's too easy to give answers, answers that may not be the answer, answers that may give us a false sense of truth, answers that are convenient but not necessarily helpful.

Life doesn't give us the answers. Why were four people killed this past week in a fluke accident? Why did Terri Schiavo have to live fifteen years in a vegetable state? Why are children in our culture abused? Why did David have to live with bipolar disease? Why did David feel compelled to take his own life? Why???

The questions are fair ones, but we may not find answers. God celebrates our questions. He longs for us to wrestle with our doubts. He wants us to share our journey of wonder, with each other and with Him.

God doesn't promise answers, but He celebrates our spiritual journey. Look at Thomas who doubted until he saw Christ for himself. Matthew 28:17 tells us that even after the disciples saw him, even as he was going to ascend back into heaven, "some doubted."

Faith has always been accompanied with doubt, and with question. And God still affirms us. David gave us an example that we dare not forget. A legacy that we must put into practice.

But in the midst of our questions, we must cling to Christ's gift of *hope*.

Scott Peck in his book *The Road Less Traveled* begins with the words "Life is difficult." And it's true. Life is difficult. But that's why Christ came: to give us hope. God has promised to us that there is more to life than struggle. There is something more to come. Life will be difficult, but in the midst of it He gives *hope*.

Listen to His words in 2 Corinthians 4:16-18 NIV:

"Therefore we do not lose heart. Though outwardly we are wasting away, yet inwardly we are being renewed day by day. For our light and momentary troubles are achieving for us an eternal glory that far outweighs them all. So we fix our eyes not on what is seen, but on what is unseen. For what is seen is temporary, but what is unseen is eternal."

*   *   *

After the sermon we sang, "What a Friend We Have in Jesus," which was the same song sung at my mother's funeral and one I want sung at mine. Everybody needs a friend like Jesus. I needed Him when David died; I need Him still, every day.

We left the church singing "There Is a Redeemer":

> There is a Redeemer, Jesus, God's own Son.
> Precious Lamb of God, Messiah, Holy One.
> Jesus, my Redeemer, Name above all names,
> Precious Lamb of God, Messiah, Hope for sinners slain.
> When I stand in glory, I will see His face
> And there I'll serve my King forever in that holy place.

> CHORUS
> Thank you, O my Father, for giving us Your Son
> And leaving Your Spirit 'til the work on earth is done.

David was a lifelong best friend to all three of his brothers. Matt being closest in age, twenty months older, had the most opportunity to share many interests and activities. They were both active in college politics, but for different parties and often sparred vigorously with their political ideas. This political wrestling, while sometimes heated, drew them closer together. We decided Matt would lead the recessional carrying David's urn.

The burial place had been an easy decision. It was the Lakeside Randolph Cemetery about four miles from our church. David was buried close to his grandparents, Donald and Dorothy Day. I was too engrossed to notice, but John recalled afterward that practically everyone at the funeral went to the cemetery.

After the burial rites, impulsively, I told the pastor I wanted everyone to sing "Jesus Loves Me," substituting the word David for me. Pastor Dan began with gusto, and many joined in.

It has been said that time changes everything, but there is a picture in my heart that time can never erase. During the singing, Matt knelt to place the urn in the grave. The day was windy and cold, making the job more difficult. There were no dry eyes as John knelt beside him to help. Together on their knees, they placed David's urn securely in the grave.

I had never seen an urn placed in a grave before. Immediately one of David's best friends, also named David, who had flown from California for the funeral, showed us what to do. He picked up some dirt and reverently dropped it into the grave. My family followed, then many of our friends and relatives, but most stood at a respectful distance, heads bowed, as we continued singing some of the most simple yet most meaningful words I have ever heard: "Jesus Loves David, this I know, for the Bible tells us so." Pastor Dan sang the loudest, with his wonderful booming voice; I with my definitely-not-wonderful but heartfelt voice sang the next loudest.

It was time to say goodbye. To commit David back to God who gave Him to us. We all lingered at the grave. Leaving was too final. We had yet to learn that you never say goodbye to someone you love.

I would gradually let go of what would never be, of my hopes for David's life and for the happy ending here on earth which I had believed God would miraculously provide. But I will never let go of my love for him. David will live forever in our hearts. David was a gift. We will always have him. He is a part of the host of heaven, and he is a part of us. David was raised in a Christian home and had a sincere faith as a child. As an adult, his natural instincts gave him a questioning mind.

I also believe and always will believe in a merciful God. I knew that day—and know today—that God is love. He would treat my son with loving kindness and take care of him better than I could. Reluctantly, we left him in God's hands and returned to Christ United Methodist Church of Randolph, the church where David was baptized, confirmed, attended Sunday school, and participated in Christmas programs and youth group. It was uplifting to see people who knew David well and who shared wonderful memories with us.

Delicious smells from the kitchen reminded me I had not eaten all day. I piled my plate high. The food was wonderful, but I just couldn't eat. When no one was looking, I again threw most of it away.

*   *   *

My family congregated at our home following the service. Food and drink were again laid out. I was exhausted but was glad to be surrounded by family. We need God and we need people.

We admired again the bench that my brothers, sisters, nieces, and nephews gave in loving memory of David.

We had run out of programs at the funeral. From my computer, I printed more copies of the eulogy, which had been on the back. I wanted to ensure that each member of my family had one, for it contained some of the thoughts that had raced through my mind during one of the sleepless nights after David's death.

Celebration of Life of David Harold Day

David Harold Day, thirty-three, died April 19, 2005, after a courageous eight-year battle with bipolar.

David was welcomed into John's and Pat Day's arms on Sunday, September 30, 1971. His big brothers Mike and Matt were so proud of him, and six years later David was equally proud when he became big brother to Daniel.

By any measure, David's short life was long on accomplishments. By nature he was curious—an avid reader who loved learning, drama, debate team, and politics. He also enjoyed training and caring for his horse, dog, and cat friends on his family's farm in Randolph, Minnesota.

David earned many high school and college awards. He was recognized for his scholarship, service, leadership, and character as a member of the Arista Honor Society, served as president of the College Democrats, and was on the dean's list in college and in law school and was awarded a University of Minnesota Academic Partnership. Later, David became a member of Mensa.

As is true for most college students, there were times when David and his parents disagreed. Consider, if you will, this example: The phone rings at two in the morning; David on the other end says, "Mom, I called so you wouldn't worry if you call me this weekend and I'm not in the dorm. I'm on my way to Washington, D.C., to protest our involvement in the [First Gulf] war." A displeased Pat responds with, "David, you would be safer and better off staying on campus and sticking to your college studies. I worry about you." David's reply: "Not to worry, Mom. I'm on a bus with a bunch of nuns."

David was following his passion, which, in this instance, meant sharing his thoughts and opinions with the then senator Al Gore in his Washington office. Thank you, David, for teaching us that sometimes acting on one's principles is more important than keeping your nose to the grindstone.

After college he worked for four years in computer analysis and networking while he and his college sweetheart made plans to marry. The wedding scheduled for May 1997 was not to be. On the day before the event, David was hospitalized by an unexpected, and particularly vicious, bipolar episode. In his usual optimistic way, David managed the devastating effects of his disorder with a delightful sense of humor and dignity. He never lost his kind concern for others in the midst of the trials his illness inflicted.

In 1998, his concern for the "underdog" led him to the University of Minnesota Law School and his specialty, public interest law. While completing his degree, he worked with public interest groups. After graduation in May 2001, David moved to Immokalee, Florida, to begin his career as a lawyer. He passed the bar exam the same year. Later David returned to Minnesota and the Southern Minnesota Regional Legal Services to represent low-income people struggling with legal troubles.

David is survived by his devoted family: parents John and Pat Day; grandmother Grace Day; brothers Michael, Matthew, and Daniel Day; and sister-in-law Kasumi Day. He leaves behind aunts, uncles, cousins, and many close friends who love him and will miss him.

Dear Jesus, the Day family sadly but with thankfulness gives back to your arms this marvelous gift you have given to our family.

David has stretched our imagination, challenged our minds, and, most importantly, blessed us with unconditional love.

We trust you, Lord Jesus, to take good care of him and answer his many questions.

*   *   *

When you are hurting and confused, you think the world should stop. But life goes on. All in my family were kind, but soon they were divided in groups of two or three, eating, drinking, and chatting.

Sharon said to me, "I remember after Mother's death, it was so hard for me to see everyone talking and eating like nothing had happened." How did she know that was what I was thinking? How universal grief is. She added, "I have always loved you, but I love you now more than ever."

Is God like that? He always loves us, but He loves us even more when our need is greatest. I believe so.

Emptiness in our hearts can be filled by words of love and empathy.

It was good to have the family together, drawing strength and comfort from each other. I was so glad Danny and Kasumi would be with us another week before flying back to Germany. The funeral was over. Now the hard work of grieving would begin.

During the following months I learned that friends who have lost a child are the ones who know by instinct what to say. They gave words to comfort, salve to soothe the wound. A friend who had lost a child as a young adult through a car accident reminded me that at baptism we give our child to God. At death we conclude our promise.

I knew at the time of baptism I had dedicated David to God. I had no way of knowing at the time how hard it would be to give him back at the age of thirty-three.

Sunday, April 24

On Sunday we returned to church. I thanked the members of the congregation for upholding us during this painful trial. There was warmth between our family and church family. Yet it was painful. So many memories of David attending on my lap, then beside his brothers, participating in Christmas pageants, saying his part, always loud and clear with a certain "presence" even at a young age. Then later playing piano and singing a

Christmas carol with brother Matt. I was glad to be there but also glad to leave.

Church would continue to be painful, but John and I still attended regularly.

We needed it.

Church is a place to be joyful, a place where you are expected to be "just fine." How many sermons have I heard saying that our praise and joyful spirits are a witness to God and our faith? I went through the motions with a fallen spirit, yet I needed the powerful message, the liturgy, the words of praise, the prayers, the comfort of scripture, the fellowship of believers, the acknowledgment of our grief, the signs of genuine sharing and concern. I learned that the less you feel like going to church, the stronger your need for church.

Monday, April 25

John, Matt, Bert, and Bob Reese took two pickups and a car and drove to David's St. Paul apartment to remove his possessions. I wanted to go, and I didn't want to go. I wanted to walk through the apartment one more time, but I didn't know if I was up to it.

Matt answered for me, "Please don't put yourself through this, Mom! There's no reason to torture yourself. We'll do it and tell you all about it." That was what I wanted to hear. It seemed right.

When they loaded David's possessions into the pickup, the tenants joined them to share their sorrow. John and Matt were deeply touched by their grief and tears over their loss of David. The building where David was resident manager is located in an area of St. Paul where the residents come from all walks of life. They include African Americans, African immigrants, and whites. Most of them are low income. David had meant much to each of them.

Jeanne and Sue Rohland, the two owners, said they would remember David always. They shared some of their memories in the letter they gave us at the visitation:

David treated each of the residents with dignity and respect. As resident manager, he was able to handle the small crises that would arise among the tenants with tremendous diplomacy. Indeed, he was a diplomat, a negotiator, a referee, a guiding hand.

We considered David a tremendous asset and a wonderful human being. He would come up with ideas for the building (he was thrilled when he found a great deal for a rug shampooer on the Internet!) and was a stabilizing influence. When we talked, it was about so many things—the apartment building, politics, the *Onion* newspaper, health, and nutrition. He was a gentle soul with a terrific laugh.

Jeanne and Sue also shared the reaction of the residents to David's death when they first told them the sad news. Each was saddened and spoke about how much they would miss David. There were tears and some laughter too. A single mom sobbed and recalled how David checked on her well-being after she had called the paramedics for her severe back pain.

Marwan, an African immigrant, cried. Betty, another African immigrant, expressed concern about David's family. A brother and sister fondly recalled David working around the building. Everyone talked about remembering David and his family in their prayers. They recalled him as a gentle and kind man with a hearty laugh.

When John and Matt returned with David's worldly goods, they delivered his books, clothes, pictures, and household items to what we call the "new basement." We live in a 106-year-old farm home on a century farm. When we added a family room in 1981, we also put a "new" basement below for storage and a pool table.

We decided to put off going through David's possessions until we could emotionally cope with it. Actually while we were never *ready* to do it, we just did it. As I pondered what to do with them, I touched his clothes, I smelled them, I remembered how handsome he looked in them. I had always admired David's taste in clothes. I remembered now how he would occasionally give me a tactful suggestion on ways to be more "progressive"—as opposed to old-fashioned—in my own fashion choices. Being of practical Scotch-Irish stock, I was glad to give his clothes to some good friends who could use them.

John's sister Karen and my sister Bernie both came to help with addressing, inserting, and stamping thank-you letters. We had fun sharing the job, lunch, and time together. Their presence was needed more than the help.

*   *   *

I remember the time of my life I felt the most shunned. Much more vivid in my mind is the time of my life I felt the most sad but also the most deeply loved: the days and years following April 19, 2005.

I was in a deep dark hole with no way out. The only light came from the love of my family and friends. They soothed the pain. They shared the loss. They loved me when I could not love myself. I would name them, but there were so many it's perhaps better not to. All of you dear ones know who you are.

I thought often of Matt's first words when he walked into the room with tears in his eyes: "We're going to get through this, Mom." Not *you*, but *we*. Together as a family we would get through it. These words echoed through my mind and helped carry me along. They rang in my ears daily. They still do. "We're going to get through this." I repeated these affirming words many times in the days, weeks, months, and years that followed. At first it was once every ten minutes, then once every hour, then once a day. Gradually I said them less often.

When Mike saw me looking sad a few days after the funeral, he said, "Why couldn't this happen to a mother who didn't love her children?" I replied, "I have pondered the same question *many* times." Wouldn't a mother who did not love unconditionally suffer less, miss her child less? Why? why? why? I asked. Every parent who loses a child "too soon," and it's always too soon, inevitably asks that unanswerable question.

I worried about Danny most of all. He had had no time to adjust to his new job and the new country he would need to return to soon. He was trying to be stoic, lest his pain hurt us. A few days after the funeral, Danny and Kasumi had dinner with two of Danny's good friends and their girlfriends. Kasumi recapped the event. "At first they sat in silence and sadness for David's loss. After a few drinks and halfway through dinner, their spirits lifted, and they started telling stories of the fun and adventures they had in their school days." With a twinkle in her eyes, Kasumi concluded, "They were bad boys!"

We continued to be showered with kindness and love by friends and neighbors. The refrigerator and freezer were bulging with food. No need to cook, just make a selection and warm it up. Each brought our family the love of Jesus in their own special way. Some came and sat in silence. Tom with his special gift of thoughtfulness often showed up unexpectedly just to be there to share our grief. Others brought soup, a book, a journal, a prayer shawl, comforting words, all visible signs that they were thinking of us and cared.

My life changed dramatically on April 19, 2005. But as I look at the whole picture, I have to wonder, was it a change or an evolution that had been happening for eight years? The beginning was bipolar. The death was unforeseeable but coming.

A single event can awaken within us a
stranger totally unknown to us. To live is to be slowly born.
—Antoine de Saint-Exupery

I Saw Jesus [1]
by Pat Day

John met me at the door.
Sit down, I have bad news
Our son David is dead.
Oh no, where were you, God?
Don't you remember?
You promised to never leave me?
I need you in this sad time.
Where are you, God?

Answers to My Question

I see Jesus daily. He shows me how much He cares about me, makes meals when I am sick or grief overcomes me, helps me find my glasses, fixes things around the house, keeps the car running, laughs at my corny jokes, listens to my problems. He wears work boots and dresses and looks just like my husband John. But it is Jesus. I can tell by his unconditional love.

I saw Jesus many times. He called me on the phone and told me to meet Him for lunch. We both sat in silence with sad eyes. I talked, He listened. He looked exactly like my sister Bernie. But it was Jesus. I could tell by His kind face.

I talked to Jesus many times last month. He called me on the phone to see if I was OK. I told Him the truth; my heart was broken. I needed help. The voice sounded just like my sister Sharon. But it was Jesus. I could tell by the wisdom of His words.

I called Jesus many times. I cried and vented. Jesus understood how I felt and made me feel better. I used my sister-in-law Helen's phone number. But it was Jesus. I know by how well He understood me.

Jesus wrote me several letters. The words showed empathy, a desire to share my pain. The writing looked just like my sister-in-law Ellie's. But it was Jesus. I could tell by the loving words that touched my heart.

I saw Jesus after David died. He came to my house looking sad. He sat with me. He brought me food. He did errands. His voice and face were just like my brother Norman. But it was Jesus. I could tell by the way he had helped me in the past and served me in my hour of need.

I saw Jesus at David's visitation as I stood and greeted friends. He brought me glass after glass of water to soothe my thirst and pain. He looked just like my brother Duane. But it was Jesus. I could tell by the way he met my needs that day and many other days.

I met Jesus more times than I can count. He came to talk and listen, brought food, offered encouragement, showed me He cared. He had many different faces. Sometimes He looked like my caring friends or my brothers-in-law Bert or Dick. But it was Jesus. I could tell by how He sustained and encouraged me.

Too often we underestimate the power of a touch,
a smile, a kind word, a listening ear, an honest
compliment, or the smallest act of caring, all of which
have the potential to turn a life around.

Leo Buscaglia

CHAPTER 2

Candles to Light the Darkness

God shall wipe away all tears from their eyes; and
there shall be no more death, neither sorrow,
nor crying, neither shall there be any more pain:
for the former things are passed away.
—Revelation 21:4 KJV

W hen the funeral was over, our grief journey began. My family and I had never traveled that path before, a road countless others have traveled before us and many more will follow. Many candles provided light during these dark days.

Swords hold within them the power of biological life or death. *Words*—just one letter different in spelling!—hold within themselves the power of *spiritual* life or death. Words given in love and backed by deeds influence our thinking, our attitudes, and our conduct. They nourish our hearts and restore our souls.

Letters—those received and those sent in response—were some of the candles that relieved the pain and loneliness we were experiencing (see the appendix). The letters from Melissa, David's lifelong friend, and Becky Elleraas, his cousin, captured David's spirit.

Dear Pat and John, and Matt and Mike and Danny,
I am very sorry for your loss. David's always been such a great friend to me, always willing to listen (and interrupt with questions!) and always willing to help me however he could and whenever I asked. I'll miss him every week

when I don't see him, the next time I need something good to read, the next time I buy art. And the next time I read the *Onion*, of course.

David charmed every one of my friends that he met, and they'll all miss him too.

Please do let me know if there's any way I can help you during this impossible time. I promise to keep in touch.

Love, Melissa (David's friend)

Dear Pat, John, Mike, Matt and Danny,

Our deepest thoughts and prayers are with you all at this time. We pray that God will be with you for all the ups and downs of emotions you are, and will be, feeling. He will never leave you.

Please know that we are here for you and would love to help in any way.

Pat and John, David was a wonderful person. I think of how he had such a KIND AND GENTLE HEART. He was so easygoing and always seemed to have a smile on his face. When you talked to him, his eyes always seemed to light up. He was so loving, kind, gentle, witty with a great sense of humor, and always ready to listen. I remember him as a great listener. I know it takes two wonderful people to create such a wonderful man, and I know that David felt blessed to have you both as his parents.

Mike, Matt, and Danny . . .

There probably aren't too many things that are stronger than the bond between brothers. I bet you all have a million memories stored up—some good, some bad—but all of them so special and meaningful in their own way. I know David felt blessed to have you all as his brothers, to call you family. Many people go through life never experiencing what you have, that brotherly bond. I'm grateful David had you all.

We carry fond memories of David with us. We love you and hold you in our prayers.

Love, Becky (David's cousin)

We discovered—again and again—that grief is both universal and so very, very individual. Comfort came from people we had not met—and from people who had shared similar losses.

This letter, sent as the first anniversary of David's death approached, by friends who lost a daughter in a horse accident, echoed our family's grief:

> April 8, 2006
> Dear Pat and John,
>   We've been thinking of you a lot—knowing that this April is an especially painful time. I don't know of any way that it can be much less painful. Not having David in your life is a daily loss.
>   I have been trying to learn to live in an attitude of gratitude for all that Sharon was to us and to others. But there is a huge feeling of missing so much—excitement, humor, joy, challenge that Sharon brought to us. Life is not as rich and satisfying as it was.
>   But, after five years, I can say the gut-wrenching pain has diminished.
>   Perhaps, someday, all of this will make sense to all of us.
>   We pray God will send you comfort, hope, and a sense of his presence—especially now.
>
>   Love,
>   Mary and Arch Leean

Resting Places, Restoring Places

> God washes the eyes by tears until they can behold
> the invisible land where tears shall come no more.
>   —Henry Ward Beecher

Why is going to church so hard after you lose a loved one? Because the surviving wife is missing her husband who is no longer sitting beside her and sharing the hymnbook. Because the mother who has lost a child is eying other parents with children by their side.

Our friends Arch and Mary Leean once made a tape in which various people were interviewed leaving church responding to the question "How are you?" Everyone sounded enthusiastic and happy. The narrator/interviewer, on the other hand, was feeling "empty" in her soul and having a hard time reacting to all the good cheer.

At the time I didn't understand the point of the tape. Now I do. For the grieving person, going to church is hard. Everyone is cheerful. Religion is supposed to be joyful, after all. You don't fit in anymore. This only magnifies your grief.

The first time I attended church again, Danny, Kasumi, and Matt were with us. It was hard, but their presence comforted me. We left immediately after the service.

The second time was much harder. I could hardly wait to leave. After church, I grabbed my friend Marilyn and said, "Come with me." She did not ask why; she read my face and needed no explanation.

We went into an empty classroom and closed the door and sat in silence. Then I talked. I have no idea what I said. She listened. She shared my grief. She did not say she understood, but she showed she cared. Pastor Dan passed through the room on his way to the second service and said, "You *could* turn on the lights." Marilyn said, "We *don't need* the lights on to talk." The humor helped.

*   *   *

David was taken from our sight and touch, but nothing will take him from our hearts. Our memories of him are with us forever. Memory triggers are all around us on our farm: the field roads where he and Buddy galloped, the barn where he played with his brothers, the kitchen table where our family shared food and ideas, the Dakota County Fair where he showed his horses and 4-H projects.

His earthly remains are buried five miles from our home, a lovely shaded spot by Lake Byllesby. His younger brother Danny did his eagle project there, planning and supervising the planting of linden and evergreen trees, which give beauty and comfort to all who come to remember their loved ones.

I love my little rituals. In the summer I water the flowers on his grave, plus the graves of his grandparents, great-grandparents, and several of his great-aunts and one great-uncle. In the winter I make snow angels on top of his grave. I talk to David and I talk to God. Then I sit on the bench donated by David's aunt and uncle, Karen and Noren Nelson. There is a small plaque on it with the inscription:

> David H. Day
> 1971-2005, age 33
> Remembered for his desire to
> give to those who could
> give nothing in return.
> Missed by all who loved him.

How much love and grief this peaceful place has absorbed.

Several months after his death, after visiting the cemetery, I wrote the following letter:

> Dear David,
>
> I love you. I am proud of you. If I had the chance, I would have died in your place. I did not have that choice.
>
> Every day I feel sad that parents are grieving as I am grieving for a son or daughter they will see no more. How sad the death of a young soldier who is just starting out in the adventure of life.
>
> You also fought your own war. You are a casualty of the battle. The enemy is cruel. Bipolar and mental illness don't play by the rules. Please don't think you lost. God is able in his time and in His way to make something good out of the mess we humans make.
>
> In the meantime, I'll carry on my own battle.

Like I said when you were my wee one,
See you in the morning.

Love,
Mom

Perchance to Dream

Friends have told me of dreams they have had after the death of a child. Sometimes they came within the first year, sometimes years afterward. Sometimes they were nightmares and they recurred for a very long time.

The Bible shows that dreams can be messages from God. I imagine they are also influenced by the activity of the subconscious mind, the amount of stress we've gone through, or possibly the pizza we ate for a bedtime snack.

Some people search for meaning or hope from their dreams. I'm not usually one of them. I feel that if your dreams don't satisfy you, there are many other sources of comfort—such as the beauty and constancy of the seasons, nature, good books, good music, and good people.

I don't like sharing my dreams with others for the same reason I don't like sharing "success" testimonies: It might be hurtful to someone who has prayed and longed for something similar. Still, sometimes our dreams have something to tell us.

I had several dreams about David. The first one occurred on September 19, 2005. The date was easy to remember because it occurred as his September 30 birthday approached and I was hastening to finish all the thank-you notes for cards, memorials, money, flowers, and many acts of kindness that sustained us after David's death and funeral. In this dream I was sleeping and David came and woke me up. I said, "David, what are you doing here? You died!" "No," he said, "that is a mistake. I am not dead, I am alive." Instead of rejoicing as I might have been expected to, I found myself worrying about how I was going to explain this to everyone who had given a gift, food, flowers, or a memorial. When I woke up, I was still pondering how this strange message should be worded.

The second dream came a bit later—and was much less mundane. In it, I was going to a graduation. Instead of climbing a bleacher, as is often done for outdoor ceremonies held in an athletic field, I had to climb a very steep hill and then very steep steps. I have bad knees (I have had total knee replacements in both legs), and I was struggling. I was also overwhelmed by the sadness of David's death. I was about to give up when Matt came up and offered me his arm for support.

My knees hurt, but the pain in my heart was much worse. When I finally reached the top, I cried. Matt put his arm around me, hugged me, and said, "You realize, Mom, David worked very hard."

I remember feeling comforted by Matt's words, but when I awoke, I was puzzled by them. Whose graduation was this? By one interpretation it could have been mine. I was the one struggling to the top, pushing past the pain, achieving a goal, albeit with the help of another. What goal? Mastering my grief perhaps?

I don't think so. The Bible teaches that you can't come to the resurrection without death. Death, the release of the spirit into the hands of God, moves us from one stage to another. In that way it can be seen as a kind of graduation.

I think it *was* David's graduation that I was dreaming about. That the upward fight with the steep hill and steps represented David's bipolar disorder and the struggles he endured with both his illness and the affects of his medication as he obtained his law degree and passed the Minnesota Bar. And the courageous spirit he showed as he complied professionally and patiently with the many grueling demands made by the Board of Law Examiners.

Yet even though I struggled with my loss, I kept moving upward. I reached the top with Matt's help. My grief did not overcome me.

I was not the only one who dreamed of David. When we came home from church several months after his death, John said, "I bet you're dying to hear about my dream last night." I sat down. "Tell me all of it," I said.

"I drove home," John said. "The yard, driveway, even the field road was filled with cars. The yard was filled with people we know. There were many of the friends and relatives who had come to David's funeral, plus some who weren't able to come because of the distance or health reasons. It all looked like someone had died. I kept talking to people to figure out what had happened and why they were there. No one would answer my question. Finally, I looked up at the window of our upstairs storage room, the window that we boarded up over thirty years ago. Only now it wasn't boarded up, but a perfectly clear window. Looking out of it was David dressed in a tuxedo, looking healthy and handsome. I walked upstairs to talk to him. 'David, where have you been?' I asked. 'I was in the house,' David answered, 'but when all the people came, the house was too full to hold me, so I moved into the storage room.'"

What a dream! I was amazed John had been able to wait until after church to tell me about it. I silently pondered it throughout the day. In John's dream, David had been wearing a tuxedo. Why? A tuxedo is reserved for very special occasions. David wore one for the first time when he and his date went to his high school prom. He also had one reserved for his almost wedding. Is heaven like a marriage celebration where *everyone* is invited? Was he wearing one in the dream to show he was in a place of celebration?

We all want our dreams to have happy endings. Though many of them do, they're not always the endings we—or our mothers—may have envisioned. I reflected on this in a poem, written before our first Christmas without David. Wondering how I was going to get through what had always been our family's most joyous celebration, I grabbed my pen and let my feelings flow through it. I began in despair but ended with a feeling of hope.

Birth and Death of a Dream
by Pat Day

The mother in labor,
Lays flat on the birth bed,
Face wet with sweat,
Waves her arm in the air.
Stuffs a pillow in her mouth,
Lest she cry out in pain.
Eyes on the clock,
Seconds slowly move.
Labor, labor, labor.
Hard work, labor,
The labor of birth.
The mother hears his first lusty cry,
Reaches out her arms with tears of joy.
"Welcome to the world, Baby Boy!
David is your name."
Mother time does spin and spin,
Minutes and years without end.
The babe full grown is now a man,
The child born on that bed,
Is ready and happy to wed.
But illness strikes,
Bipolar by name,
The road must change.
Wicked bipolar to blame.
He bears the blow with courage and pride,
Walks the rocky road, his family by his side.
But this time the fight goes not to the good.
Evil and pain win the battle over the good.
The son dies.
The mother cries.
She lies on her wedding bed.
Face and pillow wet with tears.

"My son is dead."
"My son is dead."
Labor, labor, labor,
Hard work, labor,
The labor of grief,
To give him back
To the One Who
Gave him to her.
The battle is lost,
But the war is won.
Joy slowly comes.
She remembers Mother Mary,
Who gave us her Son.
To suffer and die on a cross
For everyone's son,
And Mary suffered
Along side her Son.
The Son overcame death,
But at such a great price.
His blood was shed to give life
To all mothers, fathers,
brothers, sisters, friends,
Daughters, and sons.
So we can join our
Loved ones in that
Bright place where
No darkness, tears,
Or death abide,
And we will all see
Our Savior face-to-face.

CHAPTER 3

A Child Is Born

Can a mother forget the baby at her breast
and have no compassion on the child she has borne?
Though she may forget,
I will not forget you!
See, I have engraved you on the palms of my hands.
—Isaiah 49:15-16 NIV

"Welcome to the world, Baby Boy! David is your name."

My third son's birthing cry pierced the delivery room of the Northfield Hospital at 8:03 a.m., on September 30, 1971. When David Harold Day, 7 lb. 14 oz., length 21 in., was placed on my stomach, my body felt exhausted and weak, but my spirit was strong and full of wonder at this new life. I whispered in his ear, "Hello, David, my son. I'll be on your side all my life."

His name was chosen with care. David, just because we liked the sound of it. It is also biblical without being old-fashioned. David is a hero of the Old Testament, described as a man after God's own heart. In the New Testament Jesus is referred to as the son of David. David also made serious mistakes, committing adultery and murder. He was godly, yet a sinner. David was perfectly human. Aren't we all?

Harold was chosen because it was my father's name. Looking back, the choice was almost prophetic. The Old Testament David was a colorful and passionate man full of compassion and zest for life (just as our David became). My father, who died when I was thirteen, was caring, kind, and devoted to family. Dad was also not one to take the simple, easy answers to difficult questions, and was always searching for truth. Our David came to embody those attributes too.

My happiest memories are at Northfield Hospital following the births of my sons. Soon I would be home with three children under three and endless chores. I relished the times when the nurse brought me my bathed, freshly diapered, sweet-smelling David to feed and cuddle. I had waited and prayed many years for this family. Surely God was blessing me to give such precious and healthy children.

My joy was soon interrupted. In the middle of the night, a young woman who had just given birth was delivered to my room. I lay silently so as to not disturb her, knowing she needed to rest after her hard work. Soon we both gave in to our much-needed sleep.

In the morning, she rang her bell to summon the nurse to ask how her baby girl was doing. I was dismayed to hear the gentle but careful reply: "She seems to be holding her own." What could I say? Maybe it would be better to pretend I hadn't heard in case she wanted to absorb this scary news privately?

But our beds were close together, so of course she knew I had heard. After the nurse left, I followed my instinct and said, "I couldn't help hearing what the nurse said. Let's hope your baby is fine, and I'll pray silently for her." She was relieved to have someone to share her fears with, and we had a heartfelt visit. I learned this was her first child.

A few hours later, the nurse came to get my roommate. She did not return. When I walked the halls an hour later, I saw she was in another private room. I asked the head nurse if her baby was OK. She said, "Her baby died. We moved her to another room to spare her the pain of seeing you enjoying your healthy child."

Now what to do! Would she want to share this terrible grief alone? I returned to my room and pondered. We were practically strangers. Yet we shared a strong bond, being mothers. I got out of bed and walked to her room. She was alone. Her husband and family had not yet arrived to comfort her. Swallowing my fear, I timidly knocked on the door and walked in.

There was nothing I could say except, "I'm sorry." I held her hand, and we cried together. She was such a sweet girl, and my heart ached for her.

The next day I left the hospital with David in my arms. I was leaving with a healthy child while my roommate would return to her home with empty arms and an empty crib. I thought of this young mother often and never took my precious gift for granted.

Life on the Farm

David was a happy child. He held his own with his two elder brothers, yet tried to avoid taking sides. He was a peacemaker. Though he didn't learn to talk as soon as Mike and Matt had, when he started, he was in a hurry to catch up and practically started talking in sentences.

David was a good big brother too and always so proud of younger brother Danny, though, of course, he wouldn't show it. He was not always happy with him, however. That was certainly true the day that he, Mike, and Matt, close in age, were playing Chinese checkers. At the end there was a three-way tie. One more move would decide the winner. His elder brothers were studying the board intensely for the final move when Danny crawled over, pulled himself up by the chair, grabbed the end of the board, and pulled it off the table, spilling all the marbles.

The boys stared in shock as the marbles rolled over the floor. David looked at Danny and said sadly, "He's not even sorry."

Most events with David were not straightforward and routine. His prekindergarten test was amusing. After each question, his comment was, "That's easy," followed swiftly by the correct answer. The test administrator said to the kindergarten teacher, "There's no need to add these answers. David will be your classroom star."

One happy memory, although nerve-wracking at the time, was an instance of doing errands and dental appointments in Northfield. David had just turned six. His two elder brothers, Mike and Matt, wanted to do a few things on their own while I took David and Danny to buy groceries. We agreed on a meeting place and time, but it later became clear that we had miscommunicated somehow. Soon I found myself frantically driving to every possible place in Northfield.

The whole time, while I worried, David entertained and took care of our youngest son, Danny, who was two months old at the time. He told him jokes and entertained him, all the time keeping a cheerful and helpful manner and reassuring me that all would work out well. Which it did.

My imagination running wild, I was ready to call the police department to report my "lost" or "kidnapped" children. Maintaining some degree of calm, I first called home to see if perchance they had called home to find out what happened to me. John answered, said they had called, and calmly told me where they were waiting, a place with a name similar to that of the place I'd told them to wait.

Soon our family was reunited. It was a small mishap of the kind which doubtless has occurred in most families that have more than two children. Everyone was healthy and happy. Mostly me. That was the way things went for many years, but unfortunately not for forever.

* * *

When David was eight, he wrote this poem. I found it in his notebook with several others that were equally good, but I thought this was the one that showed the most insight into his personality. I asked him if I could mail it along with a poem I wrote for the book *Reflections from Tranquil Waters.* When it was published, it was accompanied by this comment: "Publisher's note: Age is not always an accurate measure of wisdom, as the following poem will confirm. Our thanks to this 8-year-old author."

If I were George Washington,
Or maybe even Columbus,
I'd chop down a cherry tree,
Or even sail the seven seas.
But I am not George Washington,

And I can't chop down a cherry tree,
Nor can I sail the seven seas.
So why not just be me!

—David Day, Randolph, Minnesota

*   *   *

All the Day boys had a horse. Our horses were our friends. In fact, horses were my first love. I was at least fifteen years old before it occurred to me that I might someday meet a man that I could love as much as my horse.

My sister Bernie asked me recently how our lives would have been different without horses. I was eight years old when my elder brother Duane asked my parents to buy us a horse. Dad explained to us why it would never work: We lived in town, we couldn't afford it, and in any case our horse interest probably wouldn't last more than a few weeks once we discovered that a horse had to be fed daily and watered, not to mention that caring for them involved shoveling manure from the stall and spreading fresh straw daily.

Duane and Bernie were persuasive beggars, however. My self-sacrificing parents soon gave in. Frosty, whom we modestly referred to as "the best horse in Rice County," was installed in our garage. (This was in the late '40s. Housing a horse in town, while not common, was occasionally done in Northfield, where I grew up.) I am sure our parents were praying we would all "outgrow" this interest, the sooner the better. Some prayers go unanswered. As Dad predicted, Duane, the main instigator of the plan, lost interest within a few weeks; but Bernie, Sharon, and I were hooked.

I never got over what I call the "horse bug." Horses are a wonderful and healthy addiction. Our love affair with Frosty, and many more horses to follow, enriched our lives tremendously. It also influenced the way our sons were raised. Bernie's kids had horses, Sharon's kids had horses, and my kids had horses—a total of ten, in all. All of the kids enjoyed horses for a season, but all but two eventually "outgrew" them.

It never occurred to me that a horse was a luxury, not a necessity. Since John and I raised our family on a farm, having a horse was not the sacrifice it had been for my parents. All four of our boys enjoyed riding and showing at a young age. Matt showed the most interest and rode Buddy, our delightful chestnut half-Morgan, half-Shetland pony for the first few months after we bought him. Soon after that, we bought a wonderful black Welsh pony named Smoky Joe.

Buddy was a little smaller, so logically he became David's horse. He and David were two of a kind, kindred spirits. Buddy was smart, independent, a lively go-getter, and mischievous, and so was David.

Buddy's intelligence challenged us. He liked to be around people, but he also didn't like to be fenced in. He knew how to untie ropes, so we had to double the rope into a loop, slip the end, and then repeat the process to prevent him from getting free.

He also learned how to open gates, so we had to take precautions there too, fastening a chain around it to secure it. We couldn't help but admire his spirit, however, and his desire to give his all, especially when running barrels or weaving poles, his favorites.

I will never forget David and Buddy in their first horse show in the western pleasure class. I stood near the rail, like most horse show moms, not wanting to miss a beat. Matt, two years older, was also competing. He and Smoky did a very good job but near the end of the class missed a lead. John, who never had the horse bug, was visiting close by with a friend. I walked over to tell him that I thought Matt might win. John said, "Well, don't you think David has a chance?" Soon the announcer gave the placing, and to my surprise—and David's—he and Buddy got the first-place trophy! It was the first of many achievements, including winning the pony pleasure class at the Championship Show at the Minnesota State Fair Hippodrome. To qualify for this show, the horse and rider have to have won a first place in an approved WSCA Horse Show. It was a large class, and I would have been pleased as punch if they had placed in the top ten.

Sometimes Buddy tried too hard. Once David entered the ring to practice for a pleasure class. Buddy spotted a barrel at the far end and thought he was supposed to do barrel racing. He took off at a gallop. David stood on the stirrups for more leverage to stop him, but Buddy had his eyes on the barrel. Buddy raced and swerved west toward the barrel, David leaned to turn him east and hit the dust. The result? A broken wrist, and right before our family vacation to the Black Hills.

David always had a way of making the best of the situation. In this case, that meant being a good sport while his brothers splashed in the pool when he couldn't. In his usual upbeat spirit, he generally enjoyed what he could do rather then sulk over what he couldn't.

Ponies are wonderful and smart, but the sad fact is that riders grow up and have to move on to bigger horses. David rode our quarter horse Rick for a time after he outgrew Buddy, but he never developed the bond he had with him. Soon horses were replaced by other interests.

Emerging Talents

David had obvious writing talent. When I saw a notice on a bulletin board at Randolph School about a writing camp to be held at St. Mary's College in Winona, Minnesota, I asked David if he was interested. He thought it sounded like fun. Other than Boy Scout camp, this would be his first week away from home. I hoped this switch from small town to big city would go well.

I had nothing to worry about. He had a great time.

It was fun hearing about the adventures and new friends he made at camp. There were lots of water fights. David also told me about one night when the boys went to the girls' dorms to start a pillow fight after hours but were blocked by the counselors and sent back to their rooms.

Shortly after he returned, a girl began regularly sending letters to David, all with different humorous addresses. They varied, but here is an example:

David
White Farm House
John Day on Mail Box
Randolph, MN

All of the letters got to our home, of course! Amazing? Not if you live in a small town like Randolph. David had met a "big city" girl with a sense of humor to match his!

They remained friends for years—until college plans sent them in different directions and pursuits.

David's direction was Rock Island, Illinois, where he attended Augustana his freshman year. As we left the college, I was sad at the temporary separation, but happy with his choice of future plans.

The day after we dropped him off, I called him, wanting to hear his voice. David could sense that the distance between us was hard for me. He was calm, reassuring, and full of news about dorm mates he had met and classes he would take. It was another one of the many times he would reassure and comfort me, reversing our roles.

I cherish memories of David's cheerful and friendly personality. Like most teenagers, he developed a strong mind and will of his own, but he retained his kind concern for others. While I have to admit that as he neared college age he sometimes used his verbal talent to prove his points in ways that made my eyes glaze, I always enjoyed our lively debates.

David also often used his humor to put my perpetual worries in perspective. One example is after our youngest son Danny chose to go in the army right after high school. His first assignment after he graduated from broadcast journalism training was in Tokyo, Japan. I fretted to David about not hearing from him after his long flight to Japan. When I finally did hear from him, I wrote Danny a letter: "Breakfast was very happy this morning after hearing your voice, Danny. To 'cheer me up,' David said on the phone last weekend if there had been a plane crash, we would have been notified. Like I say, you can always depend on David!"

* * *

In the family where I grew up, people were not exactly quick to agree with each other. We debated makes of cars, politics, whose turn to wash the dishes, etc. That tradition carried on in the Day family. David had strong political views; so did Matt, and they were quite different. In college each became president of the club representing the political party of his choice. That made for spirited family debates. Some might have called them fights. Sometimes, unwisely, I added my views. I don't recall our ever reaching an "agreement of the minds." I am proud to say, however, that both Matt and David would always attack the issue, not the person. Oh, if only politicians could do that.

* * *

Parents are not exactly unbiased. We look at our children's faults and shortcoming, not with pleasure necessarily, but nearly always with love. You may have noticed a hint—maybe more than a hint—of pride in him as I have recounted his story.

To be honest with you, I have to say that there was much I loved about David, but also a few things I didn't like.

He had a habit of not checking the time before calling. He never wore a watch (except at work or class) and occasionally called when I was sound asleep in bed, as he did the time he and some of his friends were on a bus with a bunch of nuns going to Washington, D.C., to protest the Gulf War. It was the middle of the night too when he was first hospitalized in Cleveland and when he called from Florida because he needed a money transfer for his plane ride home.

Yet I can also honestly say that I was *so proud* of the courage and dignity with which David handled the devastating disease he developed. He accepted it. He did his best to endure the side effects of the medication. He fought it. When one roadblock confronted him, he looked for another path. Again and again and again.

It was painful for him, painful for our whole family. Yet when I consider the whole, he had a good life. He did well in school, loved to read and explore his many interests, enjoyed his friends and his relationship with his fiancée.

You might say the illness won. It took his life. But there was much it could *not* do. It could not stop him from investing the gifts God gave him in the lives of others. In spite of his illness, God was able to do wonderful things through him.

*   *   *

David took his first step, first camp, first job, first date, and college with such confidence and joy. If you had told me his life would take a sharp detour as a young adult, I would have said, "No, I don't think so."

I'm so thankful I have these memories and did not know what the future held.

I know God will never give me more than I can handle,
But there are times I wish He had less confidence in me.
—Mother Teresa

"DAY FAMILY, 1970s"

Pat and David
leaving Northfield Hospital

John and David

David's First Christmas
with brother Mike

Matt, David and Pat.
Tip in background

"DAY FAMILY, 1970s"

Matt, Mike and David

David, 7months old

Mike, Matt, and David

David, 2 years old

"DAY FAMILY, 1970s"

Our snow angels, Mike,
David and Matt

David, 3 years old

Mike, Matt and David,
Christmas, our living room

Mike, Matt, David, John
with Blondie at Wall Drug

"DAY FAMILY, 1970s"

David, Pat, Becky and
Katy, David's 4th birthday

David, 4 years old

Christmas, David and Matt

"DAY FAMILY, 1970s"

Matt, Pat, Mike, John and David

Mike, Matt and David in
front of our church

David, Matt, Mike and Thor

"DAY FAMILY, 1970s"

Matt on Minnie, David on Happy

Mike on Happy, Matt on Misty

David on Happy, Matt on Minnie

"DAY FAMILY, 1970s"

David and Danny, Big
brother at last!

David and Danny

Pat holding Danny, David, Matt
and Mike. First day of school.

David ready to begin his
education as a kindergartener

"DAY FAMILY, 1970s"

Danny and Pat, Matt, Mike, David, John, Thor and King,
our 2 dogs

Mike, Danny and David

Matt, Mike, Danny and David

"DAY FAMILY, 1970s"

Matt on Misty, David and
Danny on Happy

David saying goodbye to
Happy, ready to move up
to Buddy

David and Pat with some of David's cousins
at Davids 7th birthday

"DAY FAMILY, 1980s"

Pat and David, David's
8th birthday

David andTigger

Danny, Matt, David and
Mike, our basement

David on Buddy, Matt on Smoky
Joe, Danny on Happy

"DAY FAMILY, 1980s"

Matt on Smoky Joe, David on
Buddy at a horse show.

David and Buddy at
Minnesota Hippodrome

David and Buddy after winning at championship show

"DAY FAMILY, 1980s"

Pat and Danny

Pat, David, John and Danny,
Halloween party at church.

David and Mom, 14th Birthday

"DAY FAMILY, 1990s and early 2000s"

David before picking up date for high school prom

David and Pat after graduation from University of
Minnesota, Morris

"DAY FAMILY, 1990s and early 2000s"

David at my computer at St. Olaf College. Taken by a coworker before we had lunch. Circa 1994

Danny and David in Hawai.

"DAY FAMILY, 1990s and early 2000s"

David and John in Hawaii

Danny and David

"DAY FAMILY, 1990s and early 2000s"

David, Pat, Matt and Mike

Pat with Buster and Chelsey

"DAY FAMILY, 1990s and early 2000s"

Pat and John at St. Olaf party

Matt, Mike, Danny & David.

"DAY FAMILY, 1990s and early 2000s"

Matt, Danny, David and Mike

Our House

CHAPTER 4

The Thief Strikes

Saturday, May 10, 1997

Life was wonderful! Our first wedding in the Day family would take place in two weeks, May 24, 1997.

The bridal showers were happy celebrations of two people, college sweethearts, suited for a long and happy marriage. David was twenty-five, his fiancée twenty-three, an ideal time to begin their married life together.

It was also a great time of year. Our faces were warm in the spring sunshine. Vibrant green grass was everywhere, with dandelions coloring the lawn like tiny yellow flags. The scent of fresh earth filled the air. My sister Sharon gave a bridal shower for David's soon-to-be bride at her home in Lake Elmo. The marriage would be the happy culmination of their four-year relationship. Their dreams were coming true: getting married, pursuing their careers, and raising a family.

Terry opened gifts with the joy and glow of happy brides. Her happiness was contagious. At one point, she and I laughed and joked about how many brides have nightmares about the groom not showing up at the altar. Terry said, "Not a chance of that!"

David and his college sweetheart lived in Cleveland, where David worked as a computer analyst and Terry attended graduate school. They had had a long engagement before their carefully planned Memorial Day weekend wedding.

Snuggling happily in my bed that evening, I had just fallen to sleep when the phone woke me up. No surprise: The call was from David; he had a habit of calling without looking at his watch. Our happy chat went something like this:

David: Hi, Mom. I hope I didn't call too late, but I had to work late to finish a project. How was the shower?

Mom: Oh, David, the shower was perfect in every way, beautiful weather, everyone enjoyed each other and the food. You two are going to be so happy. Terry will soon be through graduate school and you're settled in your computer career. How is that going?

David: I am so fortunate, I like both the people I work with and the work I do. It's challenging at times, but that's OK. Everybody needs a challenge. Terry and I will be happy together.

We had a good, long talk. As we talked about the past, I asked David if he ever regretted transferring to Morris his sophomore year. Surprised at the question, he quickly replied, "No, I'm glad I did. Otherwise I wouldn't have met Terry."

I went to sleep happy for my son and his fiancée.

But the wedding was not to be.

Saturday, May 17, 1997

A week after this blissful scene, I received another phone call from David. He was the complete opposite of the happy and confident man I had such an enjoyable talk with only seven days before. He did not sound like himself. He was agitated and obsessed with a discrimination issue at work

I did not disagree with his opinion, but I tried to point out that he did not have the power to single-handedly end work discrimination against African Americans and encouraged him not to worry about work so much. The sensible thing would be to direct his energy toward doing his job well and preparing for the wedding.

Frustrated with his manner, I said, "David, please don't take offense, but you sound so different. I have to ask, have you, by any chance, recently taken some drugs?"

David responded with strong denial. He was angry that I could ask such a ridiculous question. He most definitely had *not* taken any drugs.

Because David was displaying behaviors I had never seen before, after we hung up, I called Terry's mother, Marie, and asked her to check with Terry to see if she knew of any time David had taken drugs. "The strongest thing David and Terry have used was beer," she reported, "and very little of that. They are squeaky clean."

I decided his mood was the result of nerves. I was relieved: nerves would pass.

Terry also was concerned about David's radical change. She talked, cajoled, argued, and finally gave up in anger. They soon made up, but there was obvious tension in their relationship leading up to his flight back to Minnesota for the wedding.

Thursday, May 22, 1997

In the middle of the night he was supposed to return, John answered a phone call from the distraught bride-to-be. She was waiting at the airport to pick up our son. David was not on the plane.

John's voice was calm and reassuring. "He didn't make the airplane? Don't worry, we will locate him." Despite my husband's composure, I was deeply worried. I went back to bed but did not sleep.

Returning home, Terry found a message from David on her answering machine. He was making a desperate effort to get on the plane, he said, but he had lost his plane ticket. He was calling Terry to see if she could arrange for an electronic transfer.

She played the message for us. It was a relief to hear his voice even though I still didn't know where he was. I called David's friend in Cleveland, looking for any information he could give me. He said he'd driven David to the airport and dropped him off. When I asked about his state of mind, his friend said he had not been the David he knew. He was obviously anxious to get to his wedding but, more than that, had been extremely distraught.

In a desperate attempt to locate my lost son, I made call after call. I phoned the airlines and pleaded with tears in my eyes and fear in my voice: "I am David Day's mother," I said, "and I am prepared to fully prove I am David's mother. I need to know all details of when he came to check in. This is *very important*. This behavior is not typical of my son. He is a responsible man, and he is missing. He may be in danger. Please, please, please tell me *all* you know."

The airline employee was professional, patient, and persistent. Her voice conveyed her sympathy. "I can hear the fear and love in your voice. I wish I could help you, but because of privacy laws, and if I want to keep my job, I cannot legally give any more information than that he did not fly on the flight number you gave me."

When this attempt failed, my sister Sharon, a family therapist, advised me to call the police station in Cleveland with all the details. It was important, she said, to include the fact that David was a harmless person who was not capable of hurting another person, that he was a vulnerable, at-risk adult who must be found.

I did that. Again and again and again I called. Again and again and again I was answered with professionalism and courtesy and the information that so far they had not found him.

Finally, we received a call from a Sergeant Shanna. "We have located David. He was in a confused state and tried to enter a car that was not his. For his own protection, we took him to jail for a night. He will be safe there until his health is evaluated. It is part of our practice to check for drugs in situations like this."

The lost was found! David was safe! I laughed. I cried. Then I laughed and cried at the same time. Then I shouted and danced around the kitchen.

As soon as I hung up, I ran out to the field to give John the good news! We rejoiced together. For the first time I understood the story of the return of the prodigal son with my heart, not just my mind.

Then came the joyful call from Terry, repeating news she didn't know we had heard. David was found and had been put in jail for his own safety. She was ecstatic! She had talked to

David in jail, and he told her that all night he had dreamed of her. We laughed and cried tears of joy together. We may well have set a record for crying tears of joy and relief that our loved one was in jail!

After he was found by the police, David had gone willingly to their headquarters. The kind officer who phoned told me that even though David had committed no crime, they would probably arrest him as being "drunk." The officer called again later to tell me that since an exam had shown David free of alcohol and drugs, he was being transferred to a hospital for evaluation.

John and I sprang into action. David was safe, but it was clear there could be no wedding the next day. I canceled the rehearsal dinner. John called all the people who would be attending the wedding to inform them it had been canceled because David was in the hospital. I phoned to make a plane reservation so I could spend ten days in Ohio and visit David in the hospital.

Terry asked the pastor to post a notice on the church door, announcing that the wedding had been canceled due to the groom's poor health. Plans were made for a small group of Terry's friends to be in the church during the scheduled time of the wedding to pray for David.

The next morning David was admitted to LakeWest Hospital in Willoughby, Ohio, fifteen miles east of Cleveland. There he was tested and diagnosed as having had a bipolar episode. Instantly I called the hospital to talk to the nurse.

The nurse said David was on medication and that he was concerned and repentant for missing the wedding. He was sorry for the distress and pain he had created but still was fairly upbeat. She also told me that he had become distraught when Dr. Podlipsky had questioned him about possible drug use. This was the same reaction when I asked David if he had been on any drugs. I found this interesting and made a mental note about it. I exhorted the nurse to assure him no one was harboring hard feelings. Everyone was relieved he was safe and was anxious to see him.

Terry and I booked flights to Cleveland to visit David. I also made reservations for a week's stay at a motel near the hospital.

We would take things one day at a time. The next morning John drove me to the airport.

> Life is not a matter of holding good cards,
> it is playing a poor hand well.
> —Robert Louis Stevenson

Friday, May 23, 1997

Instead of attending a wedding rehearsal and groom's dinner as we had planned to be doing this Friday, Terry and I ended up going through locked security at LakeWest Hospital. Locked security is a precaution taken with mentally ill patients to ensure safety until the patients are stable. Before we saw David, a social worker talked to us. The young man was empathetic and gentle. I relaxed and felt my heart begin to beat more slowly. We chuckled when he told us a few of David's remarks. Obviously whatever was going on had not hurt his sense of humor or his wit.

The social worker told us which medications David had been given, explained the diagnosis, and assured us that LakeWest was considered an excellent hospital for neurological and mental health issues. It was painful to learn bipolar disorder is treatable but not curable, but we were heartened to hear that the disease was considered treatable 80 percent of the time. He added, "At this stage we don't know the severity of David's illness, but he is responding well to medication."

With lighter spirits, we went to a joyous meeting with David, rejoicing that he was safe and that there was hope. Though sobered and repentant about the missed wedding, he was the David I had always known. He was apologetic for what he put us through, but we assured him we understood.

He described to us the events that had landed him in the hospital. When he was not able to board the airplane because he had lost his ticket, he returned to the parking lot. Because of the disorientation he was experiencing, he did not remember that a friend had driven him to the airport. Looking for his car, he became further confused and entered the wrong car. "The car I tried to drive away was a red Jaguar," he said. I laughed to the point of tears. "David, you always had good taste!"

After a warm goodbye, I started for the car, giving David and Terry a few moments alone together before we left David in the hospital. Their time was short but sweet; the nurse soon came to say that hospital rules limited their time together.

Terry's mother Marie joined us for a delicious dinner at an Italian restaurant. Later they dropped me off at my motel room. For nine days I would be here and go to see David during visiting hours. Terry and Marie would stay at David and Terry's apartment.

In spite of the coziness of my motel room, my spirit felt dark and heavy. Learning your son has a mental illness is *bad news*! I needed to start accepting that David would live his life with this disease.

Soon my faith kicked in. I truly believed that with God's help everything would work out for good. I knew only the name of the illness and a few scant facts. I had much to learn, but I had high hopes. Bad news can be followed by a life of overcoming. David had always been an overcomer.

After those many sleepless nights, I read for a short time, turned off the light, and slept like a baby.

Saturday, May 24, 1997

I walked around the block and ate a breakfast sandwich at a gas station nearby, then returned to my motel room and showered so I could arrive early for visiting hours. Instead of dressing in the black dress I had planned to wear that day to the wedding, I dressed in casual slacks and a blouse.

I called for a taxicab and soon was on my way to the hospital. I have sometimes thought that cab drivers often have to be part psychiatrists, part teachers. During the trip, my driver heard a short version of my story. I suspect he had heard similar stories from people visiting loved ones at this hospital. Though I don't remember what he said, I do remember he made me feel encouraged and accepted. He listened carefully while paying close attention to traffic and turns. During lulls in the conversation, he indicated points of interest. When I paid him, he wished me a wonderful visit and good luck to me and my son.

For the moment, I was just happy to have many days ahead of me to visit David. With his talent and can-do attitude, I was convinced he would get his life back on track.

David and I had a heart-to-heart talk that day. Raised in the Christian faith, he had been curious about and studied other beliefs. I knew he had left behind the childlike faith I loved when he was a child, so in order to be understanding and respectful, I asked him to tell me what was OK for me to say about my faith. The guideline he gave seemed logical: "When the children know and understand the beliefs of their parents, saying more may not be helpful. Some need to find their own way."

David's next remark surprised me. He said he could not remember the words of the song "Jesus Loves Me" and asked me to sing it, which I did. He pointed out the song had the wrong grammatical order: "Little ones to him belong" is subject, object, and verb instead of subject, verb, and object. Quickly he answered his own question, "It is just to make it rhyme."

Little did I know that this song would be the one we would sing eight years later as we covered David's urn with dirt.

Sunday, May 25, 1997

Terry's mother Marie was there when I arrived on Sunday. She had typed a letter to David's employers which told them of his breakdown and hospitalization and explained his need to take some time off work for health reasons. David signed the letter, and she agreed to deliver it. He was not ready to return to work yet but was hopeful he could do some work from his hospital bed.

After a brief visit, Marie left to do some cleaning at the apartment David and Terry had shared. Since his room was small, David and I went to another room that provided coffee and a table with a better view of the grounds. He told me he had decided that he and Terry should live in separate apartments until they were officially married. This was a major change from his previous viewpoint, and it puzzled me. I said, "But, David, you are engaged, and you have already lived together. What has changed?" He explained, "I feel the moral choice is to be married first."

Shortly, Terry arrived carrying the Bible David had asked her to bring. This pleased me. The Bible always gave me hope. Surely it would be of help to him in dealing with the illness.

A few hours later, I left to return to my motel room and give David and Terry some privacy. That took willpower. I would have loved to be a mouse in the corner to hear her reaction when David explained to Terry his belief they should live apart until after marriage.

Monday, May 26, 1997

When I entered his room, David was visiting with a new friend, a patient named Paul. He looked to be in his late thirties and also had bipolar. Before it struck, he had had a good job and a healthy marriage. But the illness made him unable to work, and the problems of bipolar were too much for his marriage. His wife had sought a divorce.

My heart ached as Paul revealed his story to us. He seemed to be doing well, probably because he had resigned himself to this new life. Though it was not what he had planned and hoped for, it was something he'd learned to accept. He told us he made occasional trips to the hospital to get his medicine readjusted and better learn to "live with the cards I am dealt."

His story opened my heart and mind to the reality of mental illness. I thought about what I could do when I was less busy with my job, something that would help those who suffered with mental illness.

I had much to learn. We all did. We would grow in our souls from our experience, I knew, but I did not want to grow. I wanted David to live without this illness!

Still, I felt, we all felt, that everything would work out—we would just have to learn to play the cards we had been dealt. Was I naive? Ignorant? Uninformed? An optimist? Strong in my faith?

In hindsight, I would now say all of the above.

Tuesday, May 27, 1997

David was alert and happy to see me. Shortly his friend Paul entered the room, and David asked him to recite the Lord's Prayer. Paul said it with sincerity, saying, "David, this is the only prayer you need to know and say." In my head, I prayed too. "Lord, help David to have faith in you, with his feet solidly planted in reality and Mother Earth. Surely that is not too much to ask."

With his outgoing and friendly personality, David soon made friends with other patients who sought him for conversation and advice. Several commented that David was so lucky to have visitors. My heart ached for them all.

In the afternoon David was rather groggy. Nurse Joanne said David's diagnosis was that he had had a manic (delusional) episode triggered by stress. The cause of his disorganized thought process needed to be determined. There was a possibility it was only a brief manic episode caused by stress rather than bipolar disorder, which is a lifelong disease. I clung to that hope.

Dr. Podlipsky came and talked to David and me. In appearance and manner he reminded me a little of Jack Nicholson. I found him to be professional, astute, and knowledgeable. He explained the medication David would be using and warned me that a lot of males do not take their meds.

He also looked me in the eye and said, "Consider joining NAMI, the National Association for the Mentally Ill (now called the National Alliance on Mental Illness), a nonprofit organization that provides education, legislation advocacy, and support for those who suffer with mental illness and for their families, who suffer with them."

(I followed his advice and am I glad I did! My dream is that someday NAMI will become a household word, like the Red Cross and the Salvation Army. I learned very few people know what it is like to love someone with a severe mental illness. I have needed and appreciated their support, and I want to add my voice to this wonderful organization's efforts to raise awareness of mental illness.)

As I left the hospital that day, I thought about the fact that before David could leave, he would need to be certified as able to take care of himself. I wondered, how many of us would be free to live outside of institutional walls if we had to *prove* ourselves certifiably sane?

Wednesday, May 28, 1997

I had to return to Minnesota in a few days. Every day I gave David a gentle reminder of the time I would leave. Terry, Marie, and I scheduled our visits so David would have a visitor at all visitor hours and have individual time with each of us. I ate with David every time I could. That evening I had a talk with Dr. Podlipsky. He again suggested I join NAMI.

The doctor also told me that David had symptoms of bipolar illness and should be medicated for a year. However, since this was his first attack, if after one year he had had no further attacks, he could be weaned off the medicine. If he did well without medication, the diagnosis would be a bipolar attack rather than bipolar illness. My heart leaped with joy! More hope to cling to!

I returned in the evening for another visit. Paul was happy. He was recovered enough to be released. He was going to leave as soon as his mother arrived to take him home. David and I walked out with him to say goodbye.

Paul's mother looked tired and concerned. She had been through so much. Obviously the illness affected her as much as Paul. My heart ached for Paul and the dreams his illness had destroyed. I ached equally for his mother. Her dreams had also been shattered. She too had had to learn to play with the cards she was dealt.

Thursday, May 29, 1997

On day 7 David received bad news. He was informed by Jones Day Company that he had been fired from his position as a computer analyst because of his behavior while he was coming down with bipolar. (I could not know it at the time, but his night in jail would also do significant damage to his future dreams to be a lawyer.)

David had believed that blacks were not being treated equitably at his place of employment. His concern showed his sense of compassion and fairness. The illness took it a step further—into what I would call obsession.

The day before he was to fly home for his wedding, David had had a manic episode at work. Acting on his belief, he put a message on company e-mail about his views on the treatment of blacks. While David did have strong views on fairness and equality, this was certainly not his normal reaction to injustice. His behavior was the result of a psychotic episode, which was caused in turn by the onslaught of his bipolar disorder.

Before David's illness, I could have given a definition of *psychotic* by relying on my freshman psychology course, but now I learned the true meaning of the word: disorganized thinking, irrational conclusions, lack of ability to detect the irrationality. People with this brain disorder can make bad choices unless they are stabilized with treatment and medication. (It is important to be careful in distinguishing between psychotic thinking and paranoid thinking. Paranoid behavior can be dangerous as the person may believe others are trying to harm or kill him. David was delusional at this point but never paranoid.)

If David had been unable to do his work because of cancer or other "physical" problems, he would have had legal recourse to continue with his employment. In fact, his illness *was* physical. His behavior was a direct result of abnormal activity in his brain. But neither David nor I had the knowledge and ability at this point to respond to his employer's actions.

Day 7 ended with another taxi ride back to the motel with the friendly driver and an evening to myself. I called home to update John and David's brothers. I told them the diagnosis was that David had had a manic episode. The final diagnosis was not yet known, but a nurse had informed me that manic episodes and bipolar were treated nearly the same.

Friday, May 30, 1997

David was eating and interacting with other patients and now had a roommate. The nurse said the length of time to be hospitalized for a first visit to a psychiatric ward could range from one day to two to three weeks.

David seemed very good and clear. He asked many questions about the family and showed his normal sense of humor. When his brother Danny called, he asked him if he found him lucid. He told him he was aware of the importance of medication and following the doctor's direction.

Saturday, May 31, 1997

It was time to prepare myself mentally: The next day would be the final visit before my flight home.

At 10:00 a.m. there was a meeting with David, Terry, Melissa (the social worker), and me. David was accepting of his diagnosis and interested in his treatment.

I was relieved to hear him say he was aware of the importance of communicating with and following the doctor's directions. We assumed that David would be likely to question medical procedures, especially since the medication had some very unpleasant side effects, but he had a good attitude regarding taking medication.

David asked logical questions about his illness and sounded like his normal self, which made me feel better about leaving him to return to Minnesota the next day.

Sunday, June 1, 1997

Day 10 was heartrending. When I told David that in fifteen minutes I would have to leave to fly home to Minnesota, he gave me a sad look. No tears, but he looked as sad as I felt. I thought of the days when he was young and could be cheered up with a hug, a cookie, a game. Small child, small problems. My son was now a man. I could not heal his illness. We talked until I had to leave. One last hug and kiss.

I felt reasonably calm when I flew back home to Minnesota and my job at St. Olaf College the next day. David had come off a psychotic crisis, but when I left, he was socializing, seemed to be accepting his illness, and making plans. The nurses and social workers had cautioned him to wait at least a month, until he was stabilized, before he even thought of working or applying for another job because he needed time to recover from his manic episode.

On the plane ride home I was seated by a young man about David's age. He was smart, articulate, and humorous. While the flight attendant demonstrated what to do in case of an emergency, he made me laugh with his sarcastic and funny remarks. It's easy to share with a stranger, especially someone personable, articulate, and outgoing. I told him I had just visited my son in a mental hospital who had just been diagnosed with bipolar.

Immediately, he took out a book he had been reading and showed me symptoms and treatment of this illness, pointing his finger at the names of medications and at the fact that it was treatable in 80 percent of the cases. Eighty percent seemed like pretty good odds to me. I relaxed and enjoyed his company.

After nine nights in a motel, it felt good to be home again with John. That evening in the comfort of my reclining chair, I took out the list given to me at the hospital of volunteers who work with NAMI to help relatives and friends of those diagnosed with a serious mental illness. I phoned a kind man whose daughter had bipolar. He gave me clear and helpful advice and said that treatment for bipolar would be trial and error and that denial of the disease was very common.

I told him that my son had been about to be married, but instead of attending a wedding, we had ended up visiting him in the psychiatric unit of the hospital. He said that when mental illness strikes, it is usually the parents who remain faithful to support the afflicted. Sadly his words proved to be prophetic. I am glad I did not know at the time that his words would be fulfilled.

> Life can only be understood backwards;
> but it must be lived forwards.
> —S. A. Kierkegaard

B
A pearl is a beautiful thing that is produced
by an injured life. It is the tear [that results]
from the injury of the oyster. The treasure
of our being in this world is also produced
by an injured life. If we had not been
wounded, if we had not been injured,
then we will not produce the pearl.

Stephan Hoeller

Character cannot be developed in ease and quiet. Only
through experience of trial and suffering can the soul be
strengthened, ambition inspired, and success achieved.

Helen Keller

CHAPTER 5

The Aftermath

Back to Work

Statistics show that 1 to 2 percent of the population in the United States suffers from bipolar disorder. My family was now in a minority; my life changed from normal to abnormal. I was glad to return to work at St. Olaf College the next day. After the fears and stress of the last two weeks, work would offer a return to normalcy.

A few close friends were empathetic and anxious to hear about David and how he was doing. But returning to work was hard. People were working as if nothing had happened—because nothing *had* happened, at least in their world. My world had changed, however. The adrenaline that had helped me through the previous week was replaced with a flat and empty feeling in the pit of my stomach.

When I was able to concentrate, work was the best place to be. Even so, amidst the familiarity of my work, I felt, surprisingly, shunned. I was stunned by this reaction. I wanted to stand on a soapbox and shout, "My son has bipolar. It is a mental illness. It is a horrible disease, but it is not contagious. You do not need to be afraid of him or me any more than you would be afraid of a person with cancer or his relatives. Mental illness is a physical disease that affects the brain."

If David had been hospitalized with cancer or some other well-known illness, more people would have approached me, I think, and asked how he and I were doing. Instead, no one was showing concern. My coworkers seemed to be keeping their distance. Even the supervisors stayed at bay. I felt incredibly lonely.

(Four years later when David had his most severe bipolar attack while driving to take the Florida Bar, I experienced an even more harsh reaction. I don't recall *one* person asking about David's health or voicing even a casual "How are you dealing with his illness?" Since I was working as a secretary in the Nursing Department at the college at that time, this was especially puzzling. I had thought their medical knowledge would give greater awareness and empathy toward mental illness.)

Sadly, my experience was the same at my church, which had always before been a source of encouragement and support. During this especially painful time, it felt like less support was being offered.

It's common to discuss family illnesses with friends—and helpful. Everyone seems to know someone who is struggling with a disease or sickness. Being open about such situations relieves some of the stress of dealing with your loved one's sickness.

David's bipolar, however, was not something I could easily share with others. No one meant to be uncaring, but their ignorance about the disease made it difficult to share my experience. I soon realized the importance of educating both myself and others in order to make communication easier and to relieve the loneliness that often accompanies families struggling with mental illness.

The disinterest of my coworkers and fellow parishioners spurred me to learn more about bipolar and to spread awareness. I became passionate about eliminating the stigma of mental illness and encouraging research on early detection and better medication and treatment for the symptoms.

If we are to move forward in acceptance and love of those afflicted with mental illness, I also thought, what better to place to start than in our own church? I believe God loves the mentally ill as part of His family. With His help we can start to fill this need and better minister to those who suffer from this horrible affliction and to their families who struggle with them.

*   *   *

The success of love is in the loving.
It is not in the result of loving.
Of course it is natural in love to want the best for
the other person, but whether it turns out that way or not
does not determine the value of what we have done.
—Mother Teresa

Miles between Us, but Always in My Heart

I was in Minnesota, but David was still in Cleveland. Though there were many miles between us, he was always in my heart. I tried to keep in close contact by phone, but when he was released from the hospital, I was not sure if it was because he was stable and well or because of insurance requirements.

After hospitalization, David did a good job of attending to his personal affairs. He had been advised to not search for a job until he had returned to health. Recovery could take several months, maybe longer.

In addition, his relationship with Terry was deteriorating. They decided to break up six weeks after the long-anticipated wedding date. This was another blow we all had to accept.

Shortly after their breakup, I suggested that David return to Minnesota since the main reason he had moved to Cleveland was to be with Terry. A few months later, his brother Mike flew out to help him pack and drive a U-Haul trailer back with his possessions. After a short stay at home, he rented an apartment and got a computer job in Minneapolis.

David continued to be the same David we knew—sociable, articulate, caring, and concerned for other people, bright with a contagious sense of humor and a positive outlook. He realized his loss and seemed both able and willing to seek help. Looking back, I realize neither David nor our family could have realized the full extent of his loss—not until the illness unfolded and took its toll.

Like all illnesses, mental illnesses have varying degrees of seriousness. Over the next four years, we would gradually learn that David had a severe case. Even so, with his upbeat attitude and determination, he forged ahead. The next spring he started considering a new career: law school with a major in public interest law. A very small percentage of law students choose this field, as it is the least lucrative field. It was a natural choice for David as he always had a kind heart toward the underdog.

He researched college choices and chose the University of Minnesota Law School, which was then ranked seventeenth in the nation. I prayed while he took the admittance test. He passed with flying colors. David's test scores and LSAT scores qualified him for admission. (Sorting through David's papers after his death, I found, in fact, that only 240 students were accepted out of 1,467 applications received that year.) I was so proud of him for being admitted into law school.

His three years at the University of Minnesota School of Law were happy ones. David was in a field he loved, and some of our fears of the illness were lessened. Lessened, but ever present. Dr. Podlipsky had told us that after one year of stable health, David might be weaned off his medication. This was because sometimes bipolar expresses itself as a one-time attack, not a chronic illness. Since he had done well, after a year David went off his medicine—with his doctor's permission. He did well for almost a year. Sadly, it did not continue to work out as we hoped, and he needed to go back on medication.

After the first year of law school, I noted a change in David during telephone calls. His behavior was not as severe as it had been before, but I was concerned. I consulted my sister Sharon, who advised us to go to his apartment to get a better sense of things. John and I did so immediately. We suggested that he should consider going to the hospital. To our relief, he pleasantly agreed it would be the right thing to do.

At the time, he was staying in a private home shared by the owner, another tenant, and the owner's poodle, who constantly tried to leave whenever the door was opened. As we started to leave the door, being careful lest the pet escape, David turned around to tell his housemate to post a notice in case the poodle happen to get out while he was in the hospital. His housemate agreed to do that. How typical of David to be thinking of others, even a dog, on his way to the hospital!

Afterward I wondered if we were being overcautious, but the doctor said he was in a manic mode and his medicine needed adjusting. After a week's stay, he was well and back in classes.

He was motivated and happy with his classes and the friends he made.

Birthday Letters

While going through David's things, I found a letter I wrote to him before his twenty-ninth birthday, over three years after his first bipolar attack and at the start of his third year of law school. I do not have the birthday card that I sent with it, so I do not know what "two things" are shown, but it was probably humorous; most of my cards to him were.

Weds., Sept 27, 2000

Hi David,

I finally found a card that fits! Now tell me, which of those two are you going to do? Ha, ha.

I hope your birthday is special, just like YOU are special. Oh, so many memories this card provokes.

For six years I called you "my little least one." Do you remember that? I read the book *Christy* by Catherine Marshall shortly before you were born. It was about a young woman (the author's mother) who worked with people in the Appalachian Mountains. The people were poor and simple and of Scotch-Irish and English (just like us) descent. These people always called their youngest child, with great affection, "my little least one." Meaning the youngest but—it goes without saying—very special.

I don't know why, but when Danny was born and according to this logic became "my little least one," I must have called him that too, but frankly my memory is much clearer of calling you "my little least one." Each of my four sons is special. I guess each of you four is "my little least one."

Now you are a man but just as special and even more loved. I am happy you still have that same spirit I saw and loved in you as a child: enthusiasm, love, trust, devotion, humor, cooperation. Please don't ever lose it. I don't believe you ever will.

Now you have survived—and John and I have survived—your teenage years and young adult years (fun, but never easy for anyone). We could use many words to describe this wonderful journey—growth, happiness, pain. But there is one word that sums it all up—JOY, JOY, JOY! This life is too short. I want our relationship to continue FOREVER.

Do have a good birthday and may the coming year be the BEST YET. I have a feeling it will be!

Love,
Mom

A few weeks after graduating from the University of Minnesota Law School in the spring of 2001, David was hired as a lawyer in Fort Meyers, Florida. I wrote him this letter before his thirtieth birthday in September 2001, shortly after he lost his job:

Sept. 27, 2001

Dear David,

"It's nice to be important, but more important to be nice."

Finally found a card that says EXACTLY WHAT I WANT IT TO SAY!!

Wow, you turn 30 on the 30th. That is your golden birthday. In case you haven't heard, your golden birthday is when you are the same age as the day you were born. On my golden birthday I went into labor and had my firstborn the next morning.

My happiest years have been raising a family. I remember that SPECIAL year when you were home after Matt went off to school. I enjoyed so much having just you and me for the year before you headed off to kindergarten. You were always perky, positive, fun, and tenderhearted. The good news is, you still are! Another thing I remember about you is that you were very spiritual (not religious, spiritual!) and had a wonderful faith in God. One of your vacation Bible school teachers told me that this was true of both you and Matt. By the way, Mike was not in the same class. Do you remember attending the BYC (Basic Youth Conflict) Seminar when you were about 11 or 12 years old? Naturally I've forgotten a lot that was said, but one thing I remember is his remark about marriage relationships. "In any relationship where there is no disagreement, one of you isn't needed."

Our family has disagreed time and again. But one thing is constant, our love and commitment for each other. Nothing can break the integrity of family, even if it gets rocky at times.

I think I told you that Kasumi's family (I should say Danny and Kasumi's family) got back to Japan just fine [Author's note: they had been visiting when the 9/11 attacks took place and flights were suspended]. Danny said they really felt bad about the attack on our country. John told me today that Japan is supporting the USA 100 percent. Sharon and Dick left for Norway today. When I talked to Sharon, I told her that I waited until *after* they had made the decision to go to Norway in spite of recent terrorist attack, but that since she had decided, I thought it was a GOOD decision. They are staying at a five-star hotel (or whatever the rating is they give to a top hotel), and we were chuckling over the brochure that says their breakfast buffet contains 50 kinds of herring. Doesn't sound like a very good breakfast to me.

I know you already know, but I'll say it anyway: You are *important* to us and to your whole family!

HAPPY BIRTHDAY!!!

You've heard me say it many times, but it bears repeating:

THE BEST IS YET TO COME!!!

Love,
Mom and Dad

I was praying with all my heart that my birthday wish for him would come true. He'd been through so much since moving to Florida. David had chosen to work for Florida Rural Legal Services in Immokalee, Florida, in order to help low-income clients with legal issues in social security, unemployment, housing, and discrimination as well as act as an office computer expert to help solve printer, network, and PC problems. Before going there, he shared with me his concern that Florida was not as liberal as Minnesota in regard to mental illness issues. However, after he discussed his bipolar illness with his boss, he said he felt comfortable about going ahead.

Many times I have since regretted not trying to talk David out of going to Florida. He did make a good beginning with coworkers and work. However, besides working at a new job, he was studying for the bar exam, an intense examination that requires two full days of testing. He found he could not study while taking his medication—the zonked-out feeling it gave him prevented him from understanding even elementary material—so he stopped taking it for a short period. En route to the exam, he had a bipolar attack and drove his car into a swampy area. Fortunately, he was not hurt and no other car was involved. He was hospitalized at Sarasota Memorial Hospital on July 20, 2001, and discharged three days later.

He obviously could not take the Florida Bar. He wrote his office to inform them he was being treated by Dr. George Lose at the Sarasota Hospital and would also be treated for bipolar disorder by Dr. Machlin in Fort Myers.

This attack seemed more severe than previous ones had been, which is common with bipolar. I was upset and uncomfortable that he had been only hospitalized for three days, then given the rest of the week off and told to return to work the following Monday. His severe attack left him no more ready to work than a cancer patient would be following radiation and chemotherapy.

David recognized that he was not fully recovered and thus unable to handle the demands of his new job and needed work accommodation. He asked his employer for time to recuperate and get stabilized on his medication. Only part of his request was granted. David was given a four-day week, but his request for time off to recuperate was denied. Because he had not recovered from his bipolar attack, he was unable to do the work required and was terminated just two months later, on September 20, 2001.

Again, I believe that if David had suffered from cancer or heart surgery or any other physical illness not related to a brain disorder, the necessary medical accommodations would have been met. Our knowledge of mental illness lags far behind our knowledge of illnesses that involve parts of the body other than the brain.

Despite his employer's lack of knowledge, David struggled to do what he could in his condition, seeing his doctor and joining a men's choir in the local Episcopal Church. He bounced back, requested mediation, and filed a complaint with the Division of Equal Opportunity, Lee County, Southwest Florida, because Lee County ordinance prohibits employment discrimination based on race, color, religion, sex, national origin, age (forty plus), or disability.

There was no time to properly process the complaint because David was soon back in the hospital, this time in Fairview Hospital in Minneapolis. The pressure of the situation had compounded things, and his illness had worsened. He knew he needed help and called home requesting that we transfer funds for a plane home. After he returned, we realized he needed medical help and hospitalization. Christmas was only a few days away. We hated to see him hospitalized during the holidays, so I called the psychiatric wards at several hospitals for advice. John and I followed their suggestions as closely as we could, but on the afternoon of Christmas Eve David said he thought he should go to the hospital. Immediately John and I drove him to Fairview.

Most of the time it was impossible to know that David had a serious illness. This was by far his most severe bout, and the staff recommended a longer stay than what was ordinarily allowed by insurance and medical allowances. This would require a "stay of commitment." John and I went along rather than protest. We wanted to make sure David was completely well before he returned to work. The stay made possible additional hospitalization, followed by a program to offer some therapy and help in regulating his medication.

After a month, David returned to his life with his same upbeat spirit, humor, and kindly concern for others. In spite of the hardship and struggles bipolar gave him, soon he had rented an apartment, secured a job at Southern Minnesota Legal Services providing legal help to low-income and migrant workers, and was busy studying for the Minnesota Bar. He completed the paperwork for the bar exam and was given permission to take it. It was scheduled for July 30 and 31, 2002.

The bar exam is a two-day exam. I did what I could. David studied and I prayed. He passed with flying colors on his first attempt. I didn't learn that until looking through his papers after his death and discovering his excellent scores.

Another blow swiftly followed. After a couple of months, David told me that his friends had been informed of their acceptance by the Minnesota Board of Law Examiners, but he had not yet heard anything. We began the long waiting game. Again I prayed.

After about ten months, David was informed by the Board of Law Examiners that they had made an adverse decision. He would not be admitted to the Minnesota Bar. He was also told he had the right to appeal. He sought help from lawyers who assist people with disabilities at a reduced fee, but because of the heavy demands on them, they told him they would not be able to take his case. So David hired a lawyer to help with the appeal.

Then began another painful waiting game. It took eighteen months in all, during which every area of his medical, professional, and personal life was subject to scrutiny. The board wanted to make sure there was no chance his illness would hinder him. David was professional and compliant with their many requests and demands. He worked productively at Southern Minnesota Legal Services until shortly before his hearing, helping others. While he looked in vain for employment as a lawyer, he worked as a manager of the apartment complex where he lived.

Finally, a date for the hearing was set: June 25, 2004. Again I waited and prayed. The board made their decision: They said they wanted another waiting period of two years to make sure medication was followed and working.

David was obviously disappointed but took the news with courage and dignity.

On April 19, 2005, the day we learned of his death, I was counting my blessings: David had been hospital free for three and a half years by that time, and he was on a medication he could tolerate. In less than a year, the waiting period would end, and David would be able to practice law. I had high hopes the corner had been turned on this terrible illness. As many who are coping with bipolar disorder—in their own lives or the lives of loved ones—learn again and again, however, this "thief" is a subversive and persistent one. It lurks, biding its time, waiting to strike when your head is turned, your attention diverted.

There were so many positives for which I am thankful. David never turned to alcohol or drugs to alleviate his mood swings. His motivation remained steadfast and kept him moving forward. He independently and with purpose sought solutions when an attack made him unable to work again and again and again.

His efforts included:

- Withstanding the cancellation of his wedding, the disintegration of his relationship with his fiancée, and job losses
- Applying for Social Security disability while in Florida
- Taking and passing the bar examination on his first attempt
- Waiting with patience for ten months for the decision regarding admittance to the Minnesota Bar
- Hiring a lawyer when an adverse decision was made
- Respectfully and professionally complying with all requests of the board when every area of his medical, vocational, and personal life was scrutinized

- Reacting to their decision with dignity and grace and resolutely moving on

No Time to Say Goodbye

The week before he died, David came to Randolph to meet with Pastor Dan. They talked (sometimes debated) religion, the Bible, and the struggles of believing at times. He seemed upbeat when he stopped to say hello before driving back to his apartment in St. Paul. I suggested we go for lunch or a bike ride on the Cannon Falls trail. David replied, "Today isn't good. I have things to do." After a hug and a brief exchange, he drove away in his red Toyota. One week later, he shot himself in his apartment.

Many mothers like to believe that they can fix almost anything. I believed that through prayer and my concern (and worrying), David would live a long and productive life. Surely that was God's will for him. If God did his part and I did my part, then between the two of us, David should be fine, right?

But somewhere, somehow, something didn't work. In the immediate aftermath of his death, I reasoned that God didn't fail, so the problem must have lain with me. Where had I gone wrong? I usually called at least once or twice a week. Why didn't I call that week? Would it have made any difference?

Sometimes, I thought, all a person needs to get back on his feet is to hear a loving voice. And that week I had been more concerned with another problem and had put David on the back burner of my mind—because he was spirited and strong and independent. I *chose* not to worry about him as much that week. The week that David died.

I embarked on a long, painful, and mostly unproductive journey after David's death—one filled with "What if" and "Where was God during this?"

Could it be that God's will was for David to suffer and for his family to suffer along with him? During a grief meeting, I said to the nun who was our leader, "I have heard that part of the Catholic belief is that when we suffer we are helping Christ in His suffering. Is suffering 'good'?"

Her reply: "Suffering is terrible. It is what we do with our suffering that makes for good or evil in the world."

We faced a test. Surviving the loss of a child or loved ones requires years. It is a lifetime assignment. Would we be able to take our suffering and use it for good for all the future David Days?

Isn't that what Christ did? Christ suffered persecution, cruel beatings, betrayal of his disciples, humiliation, spitting. He experienced his cruel death for only a day, but I believe He suffers eternally. A central message in the Bible is that "God is love and God loves." We imperfect humans suffer when our loved ones suffer. How much more, then, a loving God must suffer when we, His creations, do.

Will the *why* question ever be answered—for me, for you, for anyone? Maybe not. In the meantime, we can take comfort that God suffered *for* us and suffers *with* us.

There's a song whose words come often to my mind. They go, "I know whom I have believeth, and I know that He is able to keep that which I have committed unto Him until that day."

I'm not sure if "that day" means our death or the return of Christ to set up his kingdom, but as with much I do not understand, I'll opt for the choice voiced by the Jewish father in the movie *Fiddler on the Roof*: "We'll leave it in His hands."

*   *   *

I can't remember if I said, "I love you, David," before he left. I usually did, but I can't recall exactly as he seemed in a hurry. David was often in a hurry. He had places to go, things to do.

One thing I do know, David's bipolar illness is now cured. Where, O Bipolar, is your victory?

One's destination is never a place,
but a new way of seeing things.
—Henry Miller

Welcome Home, Child
by Pat Day

Dedicated to those who had no time to say goodbye

The child is born
Crying loudly to the world till
Fed, loved, and nurtured.
So his body grows,
And his soul thrives.
Plans unfold.
Life is good, 'til
The thief arrives
In many cloaks.
Addiction
Confusion
Estrangement
War
Life-threatening illness
Mental Illness
Suicide.
Cutting life short with
No time to say goodbye,
Leaving broken hearts,
Footprints,

Regrets,
The never-ending Why.
We do not see beyond this shore
The Heavenly Father's face
Who gave this life to us.
He also grieves,
The life cut short,
Before He could call,
"Come home, my child."
But the Father's heart has no boundaries,
Where both Mother and Father love abide.
He does not answer our whys,
But He alone is Lord,
His compassion is in control.
He puts aside His divine plan,
In love He meets
Our loved one
With other words.
"WELCOME HOME,
MY CHILD."

CHAPTER 6

Understanding Mental Illness

Look around carefully the next time you're in a crowded public place. At some point in their lives, approximately half of the people you see there will meet the criteria for a mental disorder as defined by the *Diagnostic and Statistical Manual of Mental Disorders,* fourth edition, a resource that health care professionals use to diagnose mental disorders. It is highly likely that you or someone you love may be one of them,[1] since it is estimated that mental illnesses affect one out of five families in the United States.[2]

While many of us know, or know of, someone who has a mental illness, not everyone knows what mental illnesses actually are.

Let's talk first about what they are *not*: Mental illnesses are not the result of lack of character, poor upbringing, or personal weakness. They are not related to a person's intelligence or character.[3] Neither are they the result of bad parenting, although that notion is one that has been prevalent for decades. Mothers in particular were held responsible. Parents were either too permissive or too authoritarian, too distant or too close, too this or too that. One person who has blamed bad parenting is Dr. Elizabeth Roberts, who stated in an opinion piece in the *St. Paul Pioneer Press* on October 12, 2006, "Sometimes parenting, not chemical imbalance, is the problem."

The mental health system, not the parents, can be the problem, countered Sue Abderholden, executive director of the National Alliance on Mental Illness of Minnesota, noting that the children's mental health system in Minnesota and across the country is woefully underfunded. "We know now that mental illnesses are biological brain disorders," Abderholden added. "There is no need to blame parents for mental illness." How sad that parents and siblings have not only had to struggle to help their loved one cope with these illnesses but also been subject to unearned criticism.[4]

Advanced medical imaging has confirmed in recent years that brain disorders are, in fact, *biologically* based medical problems, that there are significant, detectable physical differences between normal brains and brains with disorders. NAMI puts it this way: "Just as diabetes is a disorder of the pancreas, mental illnesses are medical conditions that also often result in a diminished capacity for coping with the demands of life."[5]

"Mental disorders fall along a continuum of severity," adds NAMI. "Even though mental disorders are widespread in the population, the main burden of illness is concentrated in a much smaller proportion—about six percent, or one in 17 Americans—who suffer from a serious mental illness."[6]

Mental illnesses classified as serious include major depression, schizophrenia, bipolar disorder, obsessive-compulsive disorder (OCD), panic disorder, post-traumatic stress disorder (PTSD), and borderline personality disorder. The consequences of untreated mental illness for the individual and society include unnecessary disability, unemployment, substance abuse, wasted lives, suicide, homelessness, and inappropriate incarceration. In the United States, the economic cost of untreated mental illness is estimated more than $100 billion each year.[7]

A nationwide survey detailed in the *Archives of General Psychiatry* recently compared the impact of mental disorders to other physical disorders in the workplace. Participants in the study reported the number of days during the previous month they had been completely unable to work or carry out normal activities. They also noted which of thirty mental and physical illnesses, including cancer and heart disease, they had had during the past year. Transient illnesses, such as influenza, were not included.

The results? Mental disorders accounted for about one-third of all sick days, roughly equal to those caused by back pain. Adult Americans with depression, anxiety, or other psychological disorders annually miss 1.3 billion days of work, school, or other daily activity. Back and neck pain causes sufferers to miss 1.2 billion days. "If we treated the mental disorders, we could wipe out a lot of the impairment," said senior author Ronald Kessler, a professor of health care policy at Harvard Medical School."[8]

Now the good news: The best treatments for serious mental illnesses today are highly effective. "Between 70 and 90 percent of individuals have significant reduction of symptoms and improved quality of life with a combination of pharmacological and psychosocial treatments and supports."[9]

Proper screening and diagnosis of mental illness is necessary first, of course, so that treatment and medication can prevent or limit adversity. What's the next step? Education.

If you or someone you love is diagnosed with a mental illness, run, don't walk, to your library or nearest resource source to inform yourself of symptoms, treatments, and prognosis of that illness. You will be a better advocate for yourself or your loved one, and you will set an example for the rest of us, who are much less informed about mental illnesses than we are about other major illnesses.

*   *   *

The thief comes only to steal
and kill and destroy.
—John 10:10 NIV

The Thief That Is Bipolar Disorder

Bipolar disorder is a thief that strikes in cruel ways, stealing productivity, stability, and peace of mind. It can also be a killer.

IMPORTANT! Perhaps the most effective thing you can do is to help the person with the disorder get treatment. Sue Abderholden, executive director of NAMI Minnesota, has advised me that many states, including Minnesota, now have mental health crisis teams that provide an alternative to calling 911

and often result in better outcomes. For further information, contact your state or local NAMI organization. Information about services in Minnesota is available at this Web site:
   http://www.namihelps.org/support/mental-health-crisis-resources.html

*   *   *

Bipolar disorder, also known as manic-depressive disorder, is a lifelong brain condition that causes intense, long-lasting mood swings in two extreme directions, periods of extreme happiness and boundless energy (mania) and terrible lows (depression). Both affect energy and ability to function.

The disorder can range from severe to mild. The different forms are distinguished by the severity of mood extremes and how quickly the mood swings occur.[10] During the manic phase, people are energetic, talk very fast, and may have unrealistic ideas of their ability. They have exaggerated feelings of well-being or irritability. They have racing thoughts and need very little sleep, but they lack concentration. The medical definition of bipolar as a brain disorder is much easier to understand than it is to process the life changes the illness causes. The illness can toss a person between terrible lows and manic highs. The person has signs of depression during the depressive phase and because of feelings of despair may contemplate suicide. Symptoms during the depression cycle can include[11]

- lasting sad, anxious, or empty mood
- feelings of hopelessness or pessimism
- feelings of guilt, worthlessness, or helplessness
- loss of interest or pleasure in activities once enjoyed, including sex
- decreased energy, a feeling of fatigue or of being "slowed down"
- difficulty concentrating, remembering, making decisions
- restlessness or irritability
- sleeping too much, or can't sleep
- change in appetite and/or unintended weight loss or gain

- chronic pain or other persistent bodily symptoms that are not caused by physical illness or injury
- thoughts of death or suicide, or suicide attempts

If five or more of these symptoms last most of the day, nearly every day, for a period of two weeks or longer, a depressive episode is diagnosed.[12] It is important to see a doctor if the symptoms do not go away or if the person cannot do routine activities.

Bipolar I includes episodes of severe mood swings, distinct mania followed by depression.

Bipolar II is a less severe form of bipolar disorder that involves milder episodes of mania that alternate with depression. The person does not lose touch with reality but has periods of depression. Some people also experience mixed bipolar states where symptoms of mania and depression exist at the same time. Other people may experience a form of bipolar disorder in which there is a rapid cycling between "up" and "down" moods with few, if any, normal moods in between. A less severe form of this illness is cyclothymia. While most of the symptoms are the same, the depression isn't as deep and the mania mood swing is a milder high.[13]

*   *   *

Some people experience more of the depressive cycle, others more of the manic cycle. David cycled more frequently on the manic cycle. I rarely saw him depressed. However, he would be "flat" (suffering a low-grade depression) when hospitalized after a manic phase.

Because the pattern of highs and lows varies for each person, bipolar disorder is a very complex disease to diagnose. According to Michael Aronson, MD, a clinical psychiatrist and consultant for WebMD, "There's a whole spectrum of symptoms and mood changes that have been found in bipolar disorder. It's not always dramatic mood swings. In fact, some people seem to get along just fine. The manic periods can be very, very productive. They think things are going great." He concludes, "The danger comes when the mania grows much worse. The change can be very dramatic, with catastrophic results."[14]

Some days people with bipolar feel good; some days they feel awful. Relationship problems are common. Even though they do well at their jobs, they often end up losing them. The families of those afflicted with the disease can have an equally hard time. "The condition is the most difficult mental illness for families to accept," says Aronson. "Families can more easily accept schizophrenia, to understand that it is an illness. But when a person is sometimes very productive, then becomes unreasonable or irrational, it wreaks more havoc on the family. It seems more like bad behavior, like they won't straighten up."[15]

The most important thing to keep in mind about bipolar disorder is that it is *not* something your loved one can control or fix on his or her own. It is caused by an imbalance in the chemicals in the brain, so there is nothing your loved one could do either to make it happen or to prevent it. If you have a loved one who has recently been diagnosed with this or another serious mental illness, be patient with them—and with yourself. The five stages of handling the diagnosis of a severe mental illness will be similar—for the person with the illness and for his or her family and friends—to the stages, defined by Elisabeth Kübler-Ross, of grieving a diagnosis of terminal illness or the loss of a loved one: denial, anger, bargaining, depression, and acceptance.[16]

*   *   *

Sometimes kids say it best:
A three-year-old put his shoes on by himself.
His mother noticed that the left shoe was on the right foot.
She said, "Son, your shoes are on the wrong feet."
He looked up at her with a raised brow and said,
"Don't kid me, Mom. They're the only feet I got!"

What Causes Bipolar

Statistics show that bipolar disorder affects an estimated 1.2 percent of adults in the U.S.[17] If bipolar hits your home, though, it is no longer a matter of statistics or chance. It is your life. Naturally, most of us ask, "What caused this?" and "Is there a way I could have prevented this disaster?" The answer, unfortunately, is that there is no known way to prevent bipolar disorder—because the origins of bipolar disorder aren't known.

Scientists have not found one specific cause of bipolar, but they agree that many factors work together to produce the illness. Though some scientists believe that the premature death of brain cells that deal with emotion and mood may cause bipolar disorder,[18] the chief explanation for bipolar disorder at the moment is the development of a chemical imbalance within the brain. For decades, researchers have known that a link exists between neurotransmitters in the brain and mood disorders. Chemicals called neurotransmitters control the brain's functions. An imbalance of one of these neurotransmitters, such as norepinephrine, may cause bipolar disorder. Mania results when levels of this chemical are too high. Depression may occur when levels of norepinephrine drop below normal levers.[19]

Research suggests that abnormalities in the way some nerve cells in the brain function or communicate make people with bipolar disorder more vulnerable to emotional and physical stresses. Thus, lack of sleep, substance use/abuse, an upsetting life experience, or extreme stress can trigger episodes of the illness. This suggests an inborn vulnerability interacting with an environment trigger, in the way that a person with an inherited tendency to have high cholesterol or high blood pressure, which causes gradual damage to the heart's supply of oxygen, might, during physical or emotional stress, develop chest pains or have a heart attack.[20]

Unfortunately, even though research has found that stressful life events are the main cause for the onset of bipolar disorder,

> once the disorder is triggered and progresses, it seems to develop a life of its own. Once the cycle begins, psychological and/or biological processes take over and keep the illness active . . . So the bottom line, according to today's thinking, is that if you are manic depressive, you were born with the possibility of developing this disorder, and something in your life set it off. But scientists could refine that theory tomorrow. The one sure thing is they won't give up looking for answers.[21]

*   *   *

There is no clinical test to diagnose bipolar disorder—and no way clinically to predict the pattern an individual's disease will take or the treatments that will work best. Because bipolar disorder cannot be prevented, the best approach is to learn its warning signs and symptoms and, if they occur, to get treatment as soon as possible.[22]

Though counseling and therapy can be extremely useful, severe mental illnesses cannot be overcome solely through grit and determination and willpower. Because mental illnesses are biologically based, medication will be an important component of treatment. During David's hospitalization in January 2002, I received a fact sheet titled "NAMI Facts: New Treatment Options for Bipolar Disorder." It stated thus:

> Compared to the glut of new medications developed in recent years for the treatment of such serious mental illnesses as schizophrenia and depression, the lack of advances in new drug options for those with bipolar disorder (manic depression) has proven increasingly frustrating and disappointing.
>
> Currently, the mood stabilizers available for those with manic depression are limited to the old standby lithium (Eskalith, Cibalith-S, Lithobid) and the newer divalproex

sodium (Depakote). While these medications have proven
helpful for many, there is a substantial group of those with
bipolar disorder who have either not benefited from these
options or experience problematic side effects. [23]

While I have not researched all the medications available
for bipolar, I can testify that the ones David took left him
feeling exhausted, unable to function normally, or in his words,
zonked-out. He told his doctor—and me—that they made it
difficult for him to read and comprehend elementary material,
even comic books. David also told me that he felt the medical
professionals did not take seriously his concerns about the side
effects of his medication.

It is also important to remember that people with bipolar
have a mood disorder. That means they may say and do things
they normally would not. It is unproductive, therefore, to deal
with a person having a severe manic episode by trying to argue
with him or her or by trying to figure out why he or she is doing
or saying certain things. During the episode, the focus needs
to be on getting them help from a medical professional.

Jesus Christ never met an unimportant person.
That is why God sent his Son to die for us.
If someone dies for you, you must be important.
—M.C. Cleveland

Bipolar and Work

When David was first diagnosed with bipolar, I had zero
knowledge of the illness in general or his in particular. I wish
I knew then what I know now, especially about how mental
illnesses can affect work performance and vice versa. Hindsight
is 20/20, so there's no need to beat myself up for mistakes
made from imperfect knowledge. What follows is information I
discovered after his death. Advice that, in retrospect, I wish I
would have given him and that I pray will be of use to you.

Because my son had the ability to plan and handle his affairs
during his eight years of dealing with bipolar, his illness seemed a
little less serious in my eyes. He was bright and hardworking and

had been successful in the past, so I never doubted that David could still succeed, even in a challenging field such as law.

Bipolar disorder is not just something you can throw a pill at, however. Environmental factors (stresses, unhealthy behaviors) need to be considered and confronted as well as chemical imbalances. It is also necessary, unfortunately, to pay attention to societal attitudes and, when it comes to your work, to laws related to disability and employment.

"Bipolar disorder can have a big effect on your career," notes Dr. Charlotte Grayson, a contributor to WebMD. "In a survey of people with depression and bipolar disorder conducted by the Depression and Bipolar Support Alliance, 88 percent said their condition affected their ability to work. But don't get alarmed. Being diagnosed with bipolar disorder doesn't necessarily mean that you can't keep your job. Plenty of people with bipolar disorder work and live normal lives."[24]

You need to consider, to begin with, if your current job is a good fit for your new situation. Is your job hurting your health? Will it be possible to modify it to be less harmful? If not, it may be time to consider making some changes. What do you need from your job? Do you need to reduce your responsibilities? Do you need to work shorter hours or take time off? Or do you need a different job altogether?

"Make decisions carefully," Grayson advises. "People with bipolar disorder are prone to acting impulsively. Think through the effects of quitting your job—both for yourself and possibly for your family."

She also suggests looking into financial assistance. "See if your employer has disability insurance, or look into Social Security Disability Insurance, which will provide some income while you recover. You can also look into the Family and Medical Leave Act."

You need to think carefully about whom you discuss your bipolar order with and how much they know about the illness. But if your condition has been affecting your performance at work, Grayson suggests, "Being open may be a good idea." You might be able to head off additional problems by teaching people about bipolar disorder. Increased understanding can help you get the accommodations you need to be able to keep your job.

It's important to remember this too: "If you think you're being treated unfairly, there are things you can do. The Americans with Disabilities Act can protect some people who are discriminated against because of a health condition. But don't do anything rash. Research the law, and talk your situation over with friends, family, your therapist, and your health-care provider before taking action."[25]

> That which hinders your task is your task.
> —Sanford Meisner

The S-Word: Lying in Wait

The statistics are alarming—and not well enough known:

- According to the World Health Organization, more than 1 million people commit suicide annually worldwide. An additional 10 to 20 times that number attempt suicide every year.[26]
- According to an article in the fall 2005 NAMI Advocate magazine, "The U.S. Center for Disease Control (CDC) reports that more youth and young adults in the United States die from suicide than from cancer, heart disease, AIDS, birth defects, stroke, and chronic lung disease combined. Furthermore, suicide attempts account for hundreds of thousands of hospital emergency room visits and subsequent inpatient admissions. Surveys of high school students indicate that approximately 10 to 20 percent of students report having contemplated suicide."[27]
- In Minnesota, three times as many people commit suicide as are killed by others. Yet suicide remains buried deep in the closet of taboo subjects. It is hardly considered newsworthy.[28]
- In her book *When Someone You Love Has a Mental Illness*, Rebecca Woolis, MFCC, a counselor who had been working with people with mental illness for nearly twenty years, writes that 10 percent of people with major mental illness ultimately kill themselves. This rate is about twelve times higher than that of the population at large, but not

surprising, she said, when you consider how difficult the lives are of people with mental illness.[29]

- Nearly 30 percent of those diagnosed with bipolar disorder will attempt suicide at least once in their lives. The suicide rate is twenty times that of the general population.[30]

GROUPS MOST AT RISK OF SUICIDE[31]
Males
- Suicide is the eighth leading cause of death for U.S. men. (Anderson and Smith 2003)
- Males are four times more likely to die from suicide than females. (CDC 2004)
- Of the 24,672 suicide deaths reported among men in 2001, 60 percent involved the use of a firearm. (Anderson and Smith 2003)

Females
- Women report attempting suicide during their lifetime about three times as often as men (Krug et al. 2002).

Youth
- Suicide is the third leading cause of death among young people ages fifteen to twenty-four.

The Elderly
- Suicide rates increase with age and are very high among those sixty-five years and older.[32]

Bipolar Disorder
- "Over the course of the illness, nearly one out of five individuals with bipolar disorder will die from suicide, making it one of the most lethal psychiatric illnesses."[33]

It is hard to comprehend. After she lost a child to suicide, renowned singer-songwriter Judy Collins interviewed Dr. Edwin Shneidman, a leading authority on the subject, who stated,

"Although many depressed people take their own lives, many suicides are not depressed and that suicide can be, of itself, an illness, a turn of thinking, a reasonable choice, not that of a depressed person."[34]

Suicide is one of the most feared but least talked about aspects of mental illness. Some families live in constant fear that their loved one may resort to the S-word. My family was not one of them. As a matter of fact, the S-word we would have used in connection with David was *survivor*. David was someone who always made the best of things. It was inconceivable to us that someone so life-loving, resilient, cheerful, humorous, and bright, someone who could look back on his life with a sense of achievement, someone with so much to offer the world, would die by suicide.

That is not what his psychiatrist thought, however. A few months after David had his last and most severe manic attack (three years before he died), she called me at work to talk about David. She said that because his was a severe case, his illness could easily cause him to become overly excited and suicidal at any given time. There was a possibility, she said, that he might isolate himself from people who are close to him during a bipolar episode and do something impulsive, something he might not be able to recover from.

John and I discussed this sobering assessment. Still, we remained hopeful that David would beat the odds. For a long time, he did. But not long enough.

*   *   *

The unendurable is the beginning of the curve of joy.
—Djuna Barnes

Why?

What caused David's death? I've asked that question again and again, and my conclusion is always the same—bipolar, no doubt about it. His illness, which stole from him his marriage, his plans for a family, his health, and essentially his career, eventually took his life as well.

A number of factors increase a person's risk of suicide:

- Having mental and substance abuse disorders
- Family history of mental or substance abuse disorder
- Having attempted suicide previously
- Having a family history of physical or sexual abuse
- Having family members or friends who have attempted suicide
- Keeping a firearm in the home.[35]

Only two of these risks for suicide figured in David's life: he had bipolar and owned a firearm. The latter was something we had not worried about; David had never owned a gun as far as we knew. Looking through his papers, we learned he had purchased it a year before his death. We think that he might have bought it for protection after the thief broke into his apartment. But we will never know.

There were strong factors in favor of his survival as well. He was intelligent and able to plan and handle the complexities of his life, including attending and graduating from law school. In the end, they were just not enough.

Any illness can be fatal. I have had a tonsillectomy and had both of my knees replaced. These surgeries are not usually life threatening, but people have died from the complications of both of them. Should we avoid them, then? No, we go ahead with our lives and decisions for surgery without undue worry about worst-case scenarios. We must do the same with mental illness and not assume the worst. Every suicide may stem from some form of mental illness, but not all mental illness leads to suicide.

People involved with the ill person may think they could have prevented his or her death simply by doing one or two things differently. Usually no one could have prevented what has happened. "If a person is determined to die," says Rebecca Woolis, "there is nothing anyone can do to stop him or her. People have committed suicide in the most secure locked facilities our society knows how to build."[36]

Some people kill themselves as a direct result of their symptoms. They do not believe that they will die because they are psychotic at the time. A person in the midst of a manic episode, for example, may believe that he or she is indestructible. He may consequently decide to race a car off a cliff.[37]

On the other hand, their decision could have as much to do with the secondary symptoms of the illness: They know they are ill and may be for the rest of their life. Knowing how painful and limited their lives are, they just cannot bear to continue.[38]

Why, David, Why?
by Pat Day

David, I need to ask you—
I want to know why.
I ask myself,
Now I ask you.
I ask why
In my bed
In the garden
In the car
In the kitchen
In the midst
Of laughing friends.
Yet if I could see you
One more time,
I would not ask
I would just say
I could never stay mad at you
I couldn't when you were alive
I can't now that you're gone.
Gone for a while.
When I see you again
I will not ask why.
Then I will know.
I will understand.
Love,
Your Mom Forever

Suicide happens in the best of families and to the best of people. Judy Collins, the renowned singer-songwriter, wrote a book, *Sanity & Grace,* after she lost her only child, Clark Taylor, thirty-three, by suicide.

"At many times in history," she wrote, "suicide has been a solution to a variety of problems, and has often been considered an honorable, even desirable way to die; in other cultures, and other times, most recently in our own, suicide has been believed to be illegal, or immoral. Many times unforgivable."[39]

Coming to terms with the suicide of a loved one can be very difficult. After hearing the voices of others who had walked this same path, Collins wrote, "When I began to accept this terrible action as my son's path and his destiny, I began to forgive him and myself and to find a way out of the dark place."[40]

I understand. I am thankful David died in 2005 rather than a few decades sooner, when suicide was considered a sin so grievous that those who died by their own hands were not given a Christian burial. A heavy judgment indeed. Thank God, not one person treated David's death in a judgmental manner. My struggle to forgive myself was hard enough without the additional burden of forgiving others for cruel remarks.

Praying and Working for a Bigger Boat

We're all in this boat together, those of us concerned about mental illness in America and the world. Maybe we shouldn't pray for less pain. Perhaps we should pray for stronger arms on the oars. Or pray for more people in the boat. Or pray for a *bigger boat*.

Mental illness lags behind others major illnesses in acceptance, concern, research, and funding. We can be thankful that we are past the horrors and ignorance of the 1800s, when mentally ill people were chained to walls and beaten to defeat the evil forces within them. But we can do so much more. We will not do away with mental illness anytime soon, but we will make our world substantially better if we can keep rowing this boat in the direction of not only intensified research and improved medications but also enhanced understanding, acceptance, and employment accommodations. According to NAMI, doing so would actually save us money:

> For an additional annual cost of $6.5 billion . . . annual savings in indirect costs and general medical services would amount to $8.7 billion . . . . Discrimination against people with brain disorders makes no sense, no scientific sense, no economic sense, no political sense.[41]

The true meaning of life is to plant trees,
under whose shade you do not expect to sit.
—Nelson Henderson

Educating Others

People with a mental illness and the people close to them need a great deal of support and understanding. Often, however, those around them seem to ignore their struggles. I believe that many times they say nothing because they don't know what to say. I encourage those in this situation to choose a few receptive people and educate them about the nature of the illness you are facing; help them understand what you are going through and ways they can support you. Tell your friends that in many of the following ways, dealing with a mental illness is like dealing with cancer or diabetes:

- The symptoms can be intermittent.
- No one is sure exactly what causes the illness.
- There are a number of different kinds of cancer, diabetes, affective disorders, and schizophrenia.
- Some cases are much more severe than others.
- There is a significant hereditary factor.
- There are no known cures.
- There are treatments that help some people.
- The side effects of treatment can be extremely unpleasant.
- The illnesses are very serious and often have a devastating impact on the lives of not only the people who are ill but also those close to them—all of whom need support.[42]

It is also important to educate others about mental illness and suicide in general—for the good of themselves and their families and in order to improve mental health understanding in America. You might want to also share—and debunk—some common myths about mental illness:

MYTH: Some therapies can cure major mental illness.

FACT: There is currently no known cure for schizophrenia or for major affective disorders. Some people claim to be able to cure select groups of people with mental illness. Their techniques, however, cannot be duplicated by others with a random group of people with mental illness. What we can do is reduce the severity of the symptoms in many people, and improve the quality of life for both those afflicted and their loved ones.

MYTH: Having schizophrenia means having a split personality.

FACT: Having schizophrenia does not mean having a split personality. The latter is separate and very different psychiatric condition, technically called dissociative identity disorder. It is caused by repeated childhood traumas. People with multiple personality disorder go from one personality state to a dramatically different one . . . The films *The Three Faces of Eve* and *Sybil* portray this disorder well.

MYTH: The mentally ill are violent.

FACT: People with a mental illness are generally not violent . . . There is *no* higher incidence of violence among people with mental illness than among the population in general. This common myth has done a great disservice to people suffering from schizophrenia, most of whom are very withdrawn and quiet.

Mʏᴛʜ: The mentally ill are bad or evil.

Fᴀᴄᴛ: The fact that individuals are afflicted with mental illness does not mean they or their families did something wrong or are bad people. Having such an illness is mainly a matter of bad luck, as is being born with diabetes, a propensity toward heart disease, or cancer.

Mʏᴛʜ: The mentally ill are morally weak.

Fᴀᴄᴛ: Having a mental illness is not a sign of weakness. People with mental illness cannot stop their symptoms by trying harder any more than someone who has impaired hearing can hear better by trying harder to listen.[43]

*   *   *

Each one of them is Jesus in disguise.
—Mother Teresa

Each mentally ill person deserves to be treated with respect and dignity as God's child of great worth. This includes holding them accountable, for with accountability comes personal dignity. We need to work harder to accommodate the work and other needs of the mentally ill—for their sakes and our own.

When people are diagnosed with cancer, they are treated until they are well enough to return to other functions and duties, and when they return to work, there is often little or no stigma. When a person has a mental illness, in contrast, there is not always a welcoming return to employment, adding to the isolation and depression he or she is already experiencing. Loss of employment due to previous illness-related work issues, due to fear and prejudice, due to an employer's inability or unwillingness to accommodate new work needs can further compound problems, both psychological and financial. That costs society as well as the individuals and families directly involved.

Citing a Wilder Research paper, "Overview of Homelessness in Minnesota 2006,"[44] an editorial in the April 12, 2007, St. Paul *Pioneer Press* reported that a total of 52 percent of the homeless adults in this state had a serious mental illness (including major depression, bipolar, post-traumatic stress disorder, and schizophrenia), compared to 20 percent in 1994. One in four homeless men in the state was a military veteran, and one-third of this group had served in combat zones.[45]

We can't forget the mentally ill in prison or jails either. There are currently 2.2 million people in prison or in jail, according to the Bureau of Justice Statistics. It is estimated that 15 percent of this population suffers from a *severe* mental illness. This means the United States has incarcerated approximately 333,000 people who suffer from brain disorders. Professor Richard Lamb of the University of Southern California estimates that roughly half of this 333,000 should be behind bars (a drug dealer suffering from major depression, for instance.) The other half, approximately 165,000, should be hospitalized (those deemed capable of murder, for example) or in outpatient care, rather than imprisoned.[46] Holding people morally accountable for actions prompted by delusions defies common sense and fairness.

In the fifteenth century, only Christopher Columbus and a few others defied the current belief in their country that the world was flat. They acted with courage to discover a world then unknown to many. We have much yet to discover about the brain and its complexity. Because of stigma and discrimination, mental illnesses have been misunderstood and often ignored by science for centuries. Only in the last few decades has real hope surfaced for people with brain disorders, the result of pioneering research that has found both a biological basis for brain disorders and effective treatments.

Progress has been made, but we need much more. May we sail forward through research and improved medications to treat and heal the mental illness diseases as we have done with so many other major diseases in the past decades. We are beginning to realize that mental illness is not the end of life.

Are beginning to accept that mental illness is here to stay but that it doesn't have to damage individuals and society as much as it does. That working together we can overcome the stigma attached to brain disorders and keep moving forward!

We're all in this boat together; let's keep those oars moving!

If not now, when?
If not here, where?
If not you and me, who?

THE GOOD SAMARITAN

The man was robbed, beaten and left alone.
A stranger walks beside him on the road.
He could not see his pain,
He was too deep in prayer.
Another man walked by him,
No prayer was in his mind,
But he saw the pain.
Even more, he cared
And put him on his donkey
And paid his doctor bills.
Do you know the man
Who had no heart for
The helpless man's pain?
I do, I've been that man.
We don't have my son, David Day, to
Speak for those who can't help themselves.
But we are stronger than we think.
We can carry on the work of
The Good Samaritan.
Pat Day

CHAPTER 7

Mothers

As a mother comforts her child,
so will I comfort you.
—Isaiah 66:13 NIV

After his death, every mean and unkind word I ever said to David came flying back to haunt me. Large and small, they were alive and well—and living rent-free in my mind. Among the incidents I regretted was this one. A friend sent me an email I found funny which read, "Lord, grant me the patience to endure my kids and the wisdom to deal with them, for if I pray for strength, I might beat them to death." The quip made me laugh out loud in the silence of my home.

Without recognizing that humor can be funny and hurtful at the same time, I forwarded it to David and several other people. When I mentioned it to David later, I was puzzled by the sad look I saw on his face. He had a terrific sense of humor, and usually we "got" each other's wit. Not this time, it seemed. I then realized I wouldn't always be able to anticipate how he'd react to things that I said and did.

We mothers think we can fix anything. Broken toys, broken hearts. Even broken dreams. When we fail to do so, we often end up playing the "if only" game. In my case, there were so many opportunities for second-guessing.

- Why didn't I see signs?
- Why didn't I call him that last week?
- When I tried so hard to study the illness, why didn't I understand then what I understand now?

• Why couldn't I have died instead?

All these are the normal feelings of a grieving mother who loved her child deeply. They seemed reasonable when they came to me, but everyone I shared them with disagreed. As one wise friend reminded me, thinking is logical, feelings are not.

My mother's heart often drifted to thoughts of my own mother, a loving, insightful, kind, sacrificing, and concerned woman who died suddenly of a stroke at age fifty-seven. Thinking of her, I added another question to my "if only" list:

Why couldn't I appreciate those qualities when she was alive?

What would Mother have said in order to try to "fix" me? I wondered. I got some inklings recently when I reread a letter she wrote me before her death:

Dear Patty,

Your letter made me happy and sad. Happy because you are so busy helping your church, your neighbors, and your clubs. I am not surprised because you have always been my kindhearted Irish girl. But I was sad to read you went to a bar. Going to bars can only lead to a life of heartache and sorrow.

I have been shopping for new carpet and wallpaper for the living room. I don't have the money saved yet, but trust I will by the time I decide on the right pattern, fabric, and color. I still have the stores in Faribault and Owatonna to check out. Hopefully my savings from my Social Security check will be enough by the time I've made my decisions.

Luella and I are planning sites to see when we visit you in Arizona next month. I am looking forward to our trip, but much more to seeing you.

Mom

The letter is yellowed with age, the writer dead but alive in my mind. The more than forty years that have passed have not dimmed my memory of the sound of her voice, the smell of her cologne, the feel of her gentle pinch on my arm, the picture of her red, flushed face as she knelt and dug around her flowers and vegetables. These three short paragraphs written one year before she died show her busy with plans and improvements. Her project was being carefully executed; her resources carefully managed to improve her home, which was an extension of herself and her family. She was focused on the future, excited about her trip, and looking forward to seeing new things.

As a twenty-two-year-old, I remember being amused and sometimes annoyed with her advice. She didn't always seem in tune with the modern world. I often had to remind her who the popular movie stars were, the popular songs. Oh, to be able to hear her voice again.

How thankful I am for having her as my mother for twenty-four years. And how I wish I could hear her advice now. But the parent I needed most after David's death was one greater than either of my good parents.

* * *

Near the cross of Jesus stood His mother.
—John 19:25 NIV

I am Protestant by heritage and birth, yet my pain drew me closer to Mary the Mother of Jesus. I am a mother. Mary was a mother. She would understand. Jesus suffered beyond my imagination. Mary also suffered beyond my imagination. Still Mary had one thing I did not have—a chance to say goodbye.

I was angry that my son had to suffer because of a horrible disease he didn't ask for and didn't deserve. What was Mary thinking when she wept at Jesus's feet when He suffered on the cross? Was she angry and bitter at those who whipped and mocked Him? Even though she had been forewarned a sorrow would pierce her heart, surely she had not completely understood how great that sorrow would be.

I had thought I was devoted to God and that I had dedicated David to Him, at baptism and when I taught him about Jesus and God and took him to church and Sunday school. But I was also devoted to my plan of victory over bipolar—not a cure necessarily, although that would be my fondest wish, but the ability to live a productive life with less side effects from the medication. I had carefully shared my plan with God, laid out my request to Him. Yet I had also prayed, "He is yours, Lord."

Pondering this one day after a morning devotion in my sunny garden, I imagined Mary sitting beside me, and I said what I would say if I had a chance to talk to her personally: "Mary, I know you understand what I went through. You wanted to do God's will even though you did not understand it. I too wanted to do God's will. He gave me a gift also, though it took me a long time to see that."

I have many questions, but one thing I know: If God had laid out His plan for me in advance and said, "I will give you a son. He will have a terrible disease at age twenty-five. It will change his life, and yours. He will suffer. You and your family will suffer also. And he will be taken away at age thirty-three. Do you still want this gift?"

From the bottom of my heart, knowing what I know now, my answer would be, "Yes, Lord, yes. Give me the gift of this son. I do not understand why it must be this way, but I want this gift. Yes, Lord, yes! Thank you, God; you are the giver of every perfect gift!"

> Every good gift and every perfect gift is from above.
> —James 1:17 KJV

*   *   *

> Though my father and mother forsake me,
> the Lord will receive me.
> —Psalms 27:10 NIV

*   *   *

During a Monday-night Bible study two years after David's death, Pastor Dan Horn shared with us that knowing David had changed his thinking about suicide in important ways. Prior to David's death, he said, he had considered suicide a sin, incompatible with spiritual strength. He said he now believes that in heaven he and David will sit in a cafe and have a good talk about their spiritual journeys.

David stretched Pastor Dan's faith by making him explain it in ways he had not needed to before.

David's death changed me spiritually too, as well as personally. I now believe that no one who dies by suicide is a loser. I believe we need to view those who die by suicide through the tender loving eyes of Jesus and dignify them by recognizing the great physical, psychological, and spiritual pain they and their families have suffered.

> I am only one, but I am one.
> I cannot do everything,
> but I can do something.
> What I can do, I should do,
> and with the help of God I will do.1
> -Everett Hale

In the spirit of Everett Hale, I often have said, "I'll do it if no one else will." That has involved, among other things, occasionally giving a sermon when our pastor needed to be away. Since grieving is hard work, I decided not to reapply when, shortly after David's death, it was time to seek church approval to continue as a lay speaker. Below is the statement I wrote to communicate that decision:

> I have enjoyed the privilege and challenge of sharing messages with my church family, but my life changed in April 2005. My son, David Day, who suffered from a severe case of bipolar for eight years, died by suicide.
>
> Grieving my family's loss takes a *lot* of energy. I cannot go around this beast called grief; I cannot go under it or over it. There seems to be only one way, and that is through it. "Need" now drives my decision as to how best to use the energy I have left.

Mental illness is a very lonely illness. During the painful struggle with my son's illness these last eight years, I have recognized a serious need: the need for families afflicted with mental illness to be supported with the same love and concern that those afflicted with other physical illnesses are supported.

Mental illness has probably always been with us and always will be. When Jesus walked this earth, He also saw it. What did he do about it? He reached out in love and cured the afflicted.

I love my church family. My family has been touched by your love in the form of food and encouraging words when we had illnesses and surgeries. During our much more challenging eight-year journey with mental illness, there was less support.

Many books could only begin to tell of the contributions the Christian church has made to alleviate pain and suffering from poverty, catastrophes, and physical illnesses. Pastor Dan Horn has told us our Christian message is not about people fitting in. The message is about God's love. If we are to also move forward in acceptance and love of those afflicted with mental illness, what better place to start than in our own church? What better time than now? God has helped the church over so many hurdles. I believe He loves the mentally ill as part of His family. With His help we can start to fill this need and better minister to those who suffer from this horrible affliction and to their families who struggle with them.

> We ourselves feel that what we are doing
> is just a drop in the ocean.
> But the ocean would be less
> because of that missing drop.
> -Mother Teresa

In a letter to David I recounted more of the journey his death had set me on.

Birthday Letter to David

Written after His Death, September 30, 2006

Dear David,

Today is your birthday, the second birthday since you died. I cannot wish you "Happy Birthday" and hear your voice, but I can write this letter.

David, I love you. I will love you forever. You were God's gift to our family. I prayed for you before you were conceived, I prayed for you when you were in my womb, I prayed for you when you were on this earth. And I will pray for you every day there is still breath in my body.

The wonderful things you said and did surprised me many times. When you were only seven years old, you gave me a wedding anniversary gift, a certificate to have my ears pierced. An unusual and thoughtful gift from one so young. A profound gift because it was something I wanted but had no idea I wanted at the time. Wearing earrings is no longer uncomfortable and buying them is one of my favorite things.

For a short time you lived at home. It seemed one day you graduated from high school, the next day you graduated from college, the day after you were working in Cleveland. But you were always a phone call away and close to our hearts.

What joy and excitement you gave our family. Yes, we often disagreed. Somehow our wrestling and debating brought us closer together.

Thank you, David, you taught us that acting on our principles is more important than keeping our nose to the grindstone. I'm still working on that.

I remember the happiness I felt when you were found after your first bipolar attack. Did I tell you that I couldn't eat for two days, then when I got the news, I wept and laughed with joy? Fortunately, Rita Day knew I was unable to think about eating, much less cook, and brought a huge delicious salad. It sat untouched, but after this good news,

I ate THE WHOLE THING! I was as happy as the morning you were born!

I had no idea what bipolar was and the trials that lay ahead. You learned and struggled, and so did your family.

I have gone all through the reports from your hearing of the MN Board of Law Examiners review. It was so hard realizing how painful it must have been for you. I think you would be pleased that I have written three letters to the board and the psychologist pointing out errors and suggesting that for a promising lawyer, which you were, reasonable accommodation should be made for mental illness same as any other illness. My strongest regret is that I was writing the letters after your death rather than before. I cannot change that.

I recognize my shortcomings. You were usually so upbeat that I failed to understand the severity of your illness. But I know you knew I loved you. I love your forgiving nature.

John was hurting and angry that evening we learned of your death and walked through the house stunned and unbelieving. He said, "David had so much to offer. I am *so mad* at him. I could kick his butt!" I had forgotten what I said, but Bernie reminded me a few weeks later. She said I replied, "I could never be mad at David. I am mad at God! But I love God."

I know the illness made your life hard, but I never realized how hard it was. I don't understand, but how can I be mad at God who gave you to us. With the gift He made no promises how long you would be with us.

I chuckle when I think about that bus ride with the nuns when you were a sophomore in college to protest the Gulf War and called to tell me you were on your way to Washington, D.C., to protest our involvement in the (First Gulf) war. I was worried. Of course by then your dad was at my side, wondering what on earth was going on that time of night. Before giving him the phone, I said, "David will tell you what he's doing. Now don't yell."

I guess he didn't hear me, he yelled. He was worried too.

You reassured me, "Not to worry, Mom, I'm on a bus with a bunch of nuns." The good company you traveled with put my mind at ease.

I thought of the exciting trip you would have and envied you. You were young and healthy. None of that bipolar crap then. You and the nuns and a mission. You were probably busy planning the best way to influence the legislators. Having debated with you plenty, I'm sure you did a good job.

I've got to be honest with you, I don't agree with the choice you made, if it was a "choice" considering the severity of your illness. But believe me, I never judged. How could I? I never suffered from bipolar. But I did judge myself plenty. Why didn't I see it coming? What could I have done? And so on and so on. But I am at peace with my loss now. At least some of the time.

I will always miss you and the fun, excitement, and humor you brought to our home. Thank heavens Christ conquered death for us on the cross. His love is another mystery I don't understand. Since you died, I have pondered what life is like when our spirit leaves our body. It must have been fun going on that bus to Washington, D.C., with a bunch of nuns. You were in good company, but not to be compared with the company you are with now. All the saints and angels. The prophets and the apostles. And the woman at the well. And a lot of relatives you have never met. What an exciting journey you are on now, unhindered by bipolar.

Love is eternal, your family loves you forever. You know that better than I now. I will think of you every day of my life, but, my dear son, it is time to say goodbye.

Till we meet at that Wonderful Place,

Good night, David,

See you in the morning,

Mom

CHAPTER 8

Face Your Regrets—Then You Know Where to Kick Them

Not everything that is faced can be changed,
but nothing can be changed until it is faced.
—James Baldwin

As a mother, I wanted to believe that "love conquers all." With this came unrealistic ideas of my own power. I hadn't yet learned how much "the thief" named bipolar could steal and control. I hadn't yet learned the many ways it torments those with the illness and robs their families of their peace of mind.

I remember watching a TV show where people making a religious pilgrimage were beating themselves bloody with whips to atone for sins they committed. I was horrified and repelled. Why would anyone torture himself? Yet after David died, I did just that. I tortured myself, not with whips, but with verbal abuse and regrets. I clung to my regrets and let them depress and weaken me. In the one role I most wanted to succeed, being a mother, I felt like a complete failure. The beating I gave myself hurt almost as much as an actual one would have.

Part of my grieving required facing my regrets.

First Regret

When David showed his first symptoms at age twenty-five, shortly before his wedding, I asked my sisters for advice. Sharon said to stay calm; Bernie said to fly out to see him. If I had flown to Cleveland, would the full-blown attack have been averted? Would he have gotten to the wedding? At the time I was afraid if I flew out, I might create more problems than help. I convinced myself that David was a competent person and could handle this task on his own.

Next Regret

When David called with his concern that Florida was less lenient with accommodation of mental illness than Minnesota, I suggested he call his new boss and discuss his disability further. His boss assured David that he understood the illness, believed David was well qualified, and wanted him to join his staff.

Should I have strongly urged him to not accept the job if he had qualms? Would it have made a difference? But I was uncertain myself as to what the best course would be. Perhaps I was expressing normal apprehension before David made a big transition. When we had our final goodbyes and hugs as he prepared to drive to Florida, it was obvious he was excited about his trip and the new job. After his move, every phone call was upbeat. And he seemed to be adjusting to his work well. He was busy studying for the bar and enjoying his colleagues. John and I felt good about his decision.

Then, on August 1, I returned from an outing with seven friends. John met me at the door with horrible news. Bipolar had struck again. John said, "David was in a car accident on his way to take the bar exam," one most likely caused by the onset of a severe manic episode. The nurse had explained to John that David might have thought the car could drive itself, with the result that the car ended up in a swamp.

Next Regret

When David returned to work in Florida after the breakdown, why didn't I demand, rather than suggest, that he come home so he would not have to deal with the stress of a new job when he apparently was not fully recovered? Would time away from stress have lessened, or even prevented, his next attack? He did receive some work accommodation, but not as much as he needed, considering the severity of the attack. I detected from phone conversations that he was not fully recovered, but from a distance I could not sense the severity of his illness.

Next Regret

When David was hospitalized from late December 2001 to January 2002, hospital personnel suggested that a "stay of commitment" would give him more time in the hospital and more treatment to ensure he was fully recovered and stabilized with his medication.

Without the stay, David would have been discharged from the hospital as soon as his insurance ran out. We wanted to be sure he was recovered and stable before leaving the hospital, so we did not fight it. While his health was our foremost concern, we were also cognizant of the effect commitment might have on his law career. I called the social worker to check if it would pose problems for his law career in the future and was assured it would not. That proved, unfortunately, to be wrong.

In July 2002, five months after David was released from the hospital following his worst and final bipolar attack, he passed the two-day Minnesota State Bar Examination—on his first attempt—with flying colors: he earned a scaled score of 119 (85 was passing) and a raw score of 38. However, official admittance to the bar also requires a passing score on the character and fitness investigation. The stay of commitment turned out to be a red flag that delayed approval. A long period followed of waiting, waiting, waiting for the board's decision regarding whether he would be admitted to the bar. On April 22, 2003, he received a letter conveying their adverse decision. What a stressful period that must have been for him!

"You can't fight town hall." You can appeal, though if you're going to wrangle with the Minnesota Board of Law Examiners, you're well advised to hire a lawyer. David found one who felt optimistic about his being admitted. Then there was another period of waiting, waiting, waiting until the date was set for his hearing: June 25, 2004, nearly two years after he passed the exam.

At the hearing, the board decided to require another period of two years of medical compliance and good health before formally admitting him. Again we were extremely disappointed, but since David had been in good health and stable for the past several years, we felt optimistic he would be admitted at that time. He had endured the stressful waiting period till then. We assumed he could do it again. However, the fact that the stay of commitment had played a major role in the delay made me wonder if we should have fought it at the time it was recommended.

Next Regret

Had I done enough to help him with his appeal? David had told me about several damaging errors in the paperwork, among them that he had been involved in two accidents because of his illness, which was not true. He was involved in just one accident due to bipolar. I tried to follow the process and offered to write some letters to clarify the errors. But neither David nor I followed through on that. I will never know if it would have made a difference.

My Most Painful Regret

After David's death, I beat myself up that I had not phoned more often and made sure he was safe. I do recall a few instances when he seemed stressed, but I certainly had not sensed evidence of extreme disappointment and anguish. Perhaps I would have noticed had I called more to check in.

To be fair to myself and others who might harbor the same regret, David had always been self-sufficient and competent in matters like finances, finding housing, employment, friends and associates, and healthy hobbies. I considered him capable of handling nearly everything on his own. It occurred to me that offering to help would make him feel less self-sufficient and intrude on his independence.

We were all shocked when David ended his life on April 19, 2005.

> Every man must do two things alone.
> He must do his own believing and his own dying.
> —Martin Luther

Going Forward, Not Backward

After the funeral, John in his logical, organized manner mailed out the death certificates, paid bills, and arranged David's belongings in our basement. I sorted David's clothes and gave away most of them to good friends. Then I turned to the box labeled in big black letters "Board of Law Examiners." It contained reams of information on the review that occupied so much of the last months of David's life.

I did not attend the hearing, but after David's death, I scrutinized the transcript of proceedings with a fine-tooth comb. This was a labor of love and sorrow, a painful process of thinking and feeling the stress and pain he endured as every area of his private life was laid open to their scrutiny. Words cannot express the pain it gave me. Yet I had to do it.

I was surprised at the number of errors of fact and interpretation I found. Even typical manic behavior during his first attack was not treated fairly. Considering the time frame and the nature of his illness, his getting into the wrong car (which he thought at the time was his) did not constitute criminal behavior. His only crime was having a horrible disease.

I was angry at the board for rejecting David. These feelings subsided over time, tempered by the counsel of family and friends and by logic. Every member of the Bar of Law Review is undoubtedly an intelligent, highly educated person who has achieved much. Each of them had the desire to do the right thing, but they were ignorant about the situation and about mental illness and about what could be done. Just as I had been when David had his first bipolar attack. But I wanted to learn.

I have learned much more about mental illness than I had any desire to know before it invaded my family. I will never forget the things David taught me. One was the difference between ignorant and dumb. My son told me, "Some people know nothing about something; they are ignorant. But then there are people who know nothing about something but think they know a lot. Those people are dumb. You may be ignorant on some things, Mom, but you are never dumb." All of us are ignorant about some things. While ignorance is not always harmful, being dumb can be dangerous. I decided that I wanted to be neither ignorant nor dumb on the issue of bipolar. So I educated myself during his illness and after his death tried to educate others as well.

As I read the record of his appeal, I was overwhelmed with the long devastating process David had undergone. It would have been painful for anyone, with or without the stress and pain of bipolar and the isolation it brings. David had expressed to me and in writing to the Minnesota Board of Law Examiners his reluctance to turn all his medical records over to the board since they lacked medical knowledge on mental illness. I believe the trial and the decision by the board confirmed his fears. Frontline experience would have given the board and the psychologist a different perspective and compassion. Yet, I never heard him express anger or animosity toward any of the people involved.

> Every time you smile at a person,
> it is a beautiful thing.
> —Mother Teresa

After David's death, I wanted to act with the same spirit of forgiveness and goodwill that he had showed during this process.

I respected the job the Board of Law Examiners had to do. On the other hand, I also felt I had a job to do—to not only correct the errors I found, but also do what I could for future David Days seeking a career in law or any other field.

John and I sent a letter to the Board of Law Examiners in December 2005, noting in it that it was sent not "in the tone of recrimination but in the hopes that future candidates with a mental illness who pass the bar and are later denied admission because of mental illness and related problems will be treated with dignity and respect." We detailed the inaccuracies and omissions we perceived in the materials the board had compiled and reviewed. We countered conclusions drawn by the psychologist who interviewed him with our own experience and that of every person who knew David on a long-term basis, who testified that he was a giving, caring, and unselfish person.

We concluded by expressing the hope that "positive things can come from David's painful experiences. All of us have the ability to move Minnesota forward in acceptance of mental illness and appreciation of the gifts and contributions the mentally ill can give when treated with fairness and compassion. We hope that the mistakes in the manner David's case was handled will not be repeated in the future. Let us go forward, not backward."

At the very end of the letter we shared how, after the hearing, David had told us that it had been extremely stressful, but that one member had had compassion and looked at him and smiled. We wrote, "If you know who this was (or if perchance you are that person), *please thank her for us. Let us be kind to each other while there is still time.*"

In its reply to us, the Minnesota Board of Law Examiners expressed its sympathy for our loss and commended David for conducting himself in a professional manner in every respect. It did not, however, address any of the issues we had raised.

In a second letter, we posed the question "Has anything been learned from this experience that will influence the way you will treat the future David Days that cross your path?" We expressed that our intent was not restitution but an increased awareness of bipolar that would foster fairness and compassion for the mentally ill.

In a third letter, we thanked the board for the copy it had sent us of the brochure "Character and Fitness for Admission to the Bar" and added, "David had displayed potential to be a good lawyer with reasonable accommodation for his illness. There were many areas in which he could have shined . . . . A limited work provision could have enabled David to pursue a career, use his talents and education, while protecting the public. Please consider this suggestion." There our correspondence ended.

*   *   *

Knowing that parents are probably the most biased people in the world where their children are concerned, I shared our first letter to the Board of Law Examiners with my sister-in-law, Helen Temple, seeking her insight and wisdom. I received it in the following letter:

Dear Pat,

I couldn't find my first reply to you, so maybe it wasn't supposed to reach you!!!! However, I then went and printed off your letter so I could read it again in quiet with feet up and coffee cup at hand.

How can one give feedback on something so emotionally charged as your whole situation is?? The first thing that struck me was a mother's attempt to cope with tragedy and look for anything that might have affected the tragic outcome. Can we ever see anything except from our own point of view?? In the errors that you quoted, had they not been there, would that have influenced the outcome?

Your most telling point (to me) was your desire to see those with mental illness treated with compassion and humanity. I guess the only way you could evaluate adequately how they treated David would have been to be there.

How will this group receive that letter? God only knows. Maybe that is not as important as making the opportunity to express what is on your heart and mind. I thought as I read your letter you tried not to lay blame except maybe in the case of the psychologist who gave a subjective opinion, and his interaction with David was undoubtedly the way he saw it. Wasn't it Pilate who said, "What is truth?" We parents (and I include all of us) love our children so much that when they hurt, we hurt almost more, and our window on truth where they are concerned is so much larger than a group of people who haven't known them could possibly have. We are not blind, we can see their faults, but their virtues so outweigh them that the balance, seen with the eyes of love, puts faults in shadow.

Inasmuch as we can see something that needs to be corrected, and that we maybe can help to correct it, then introspection is of value. "God grant me the serenity to accept the things I cannot change, the courage to change the things I can (and should), and the wisdom to know the difference."

David had so much possibility, so much promise that in all of our eyes that far outweighed his bipolar problem. How does one handle the death of a dream?? I have no answer. That particular dream has ended, there is no use pretending that it hasn't, but it is not the end of all dreams. In honor of David's memory, you must get another dream in order to not let his life go to waste. Honestly, in my opinion, that is the direction you are going whether you are aware of it yet or not. I won't even suggest what I see; I am no prophet, just someone who loves you very much.

When we talked on the phone, you touched on your feelings of guilt—that somehow you should have been able to do more, should have been able to prevent this. Not real. I see that you and John did so much to help, maybe more than most of us could. Have you been perfect? (In my eyes yes, but then my vision isn't very good—ha.)

Forgiving yourself is a whopper because we blow our own faults up so huge, but it can be done. Takes time, practice, and finding a way to turn it into love and compassion where it needs most to be directed. When you get your sorrow under control and not let it control you (as I think it does occasionally), you will again be free to be what you were created to be.

If you have found in your reading anyone who has been able to make sense of tragedy, please recommend him or her to me. The closest I have been able to come is the saying "Life is not fair, and the sooner we realize that, the better we can cope with it"—but in the face of real sorrow, that is quite inadequate.

One time, years ago, when Norman had been injured in an auto accident and had that broken vertebrae and rotator cuff, he was talking with a pastor at North Heights who had been in a bad accident. I think the subject was "why do these things happen," and Norman indicated he asked God that question. The pastor smiled and said, "You didn't get an answer, did you?"

Right now I know something you don't at this time. You WILL get through this successfully. You may find some of your long-held beliefs changing, but be patient with yourself, God will still love you!! With the excellent brain you were created with, and your many abilities, you have so much to offer, and one thing will be to share with others.

None of us have all the answers, but we can share what little we have and just maybe it will be what someone else needs. We are all vulnerable and weak, so I think one of our callings is to help others to stand. But all we can do is help, with no guaranteed outcome.

You have helped me, Pat. One area I think of right now is that you challenge me to reject platitudes and search for the real. I fail often, but will keep trying!!!

I will entrust this to snail mail since my other letter didn't go through.

Love, Helen

*   *   *

What We Do with Our Suffering

Does God teach us through our suffering as well as through our triumphs and joy? Earlier I mentioned a grief meeting where I asked a nun the question "Is suffering 'good'? Is its purpose to enable us to help share the load of Christ's suffering? Where does it fit into God's plan?" Her reply: "Suffering is horrible. It is what we do with our suffering that makes for the difference between good and evil in the world."

Her answer may not answer my questions or your questions on the subject of suffering, but it did satisfy me at the time. In her vocation, I am sure, she witnessed much suffering and worked to share the burden. The verse that went through my mind repeatedly and became almost a mantra was the one that my mother had had me write out several times on 3 × 5 inch recipe cards and tape to several prominent places in our house. This was my mother's way. She didn't preach or quote scripture, but without comment gave me a household chore. The card said,

Bear ye one another's burdens and so fulfill the law of Christ.
—Galatians 6:2 KJV

That is what Jesus did for us. He bore our sin burden and suffered in many ways the same problems, disappointments, and sadness that we do. The book of Hebrews tells us that He experienced everything we suffer. Since He did not have biological children, I doubted that he suffered alongside a child with mental illness and the ravages it brings. Yet we *are* His children, biological or not. He became like us. He understands. He became like us that we may become like Him.

When I taught Sunday school, I tried to focus on Christ. God loved us so much that he gave His Son to die in payment for our sins. Sounds simple. I think most of the fourth graders got the message.

Yet I never understood the cost until I lost my son. How could God love us *that* much? I love a lot of people, but if I were asked to give the life of one of my sons for one of them, I wouldn't have to think more than a split second before saying, "No way!"

Jesus loved us enough to suffer a painful death for us. Jesus in his humanness was sorrowful and asked His Father to remove the cross from Him. He wrestled in the garden before His arrest. He desired human comfort during these hours and asked Peter, James, and John to watch and pray with him. The disciples he chose were very human and very tired. Jesus returned to them three times and found them asleep. Jesus had told them He would die and live again. Yet after His death, they showed they didn't understand and were not ready to face it.

I was unprepared for David's death. I was unable to prevent it. We can all take comfort from the simple but beautiful children's hymn David and I sang at the hospital when he was first diagnosed with bipolar and which was also sung spontaneously at David's burial:

Jesus loves me,
This I know.
For the Bible
Tells me so.

Little ones
(and aren't we all His "little ones?")
To Him belong.
They are weak,
But He is strong.

Forgiveness Gives the Hardest Kick

There is a positive side to anger, writes Dr. Rachel Remen, citing cancer studies that suggest that many people who recover become angry first. Anger is a strong desire for things to be different, a demand for change. It may be the first expression of the will to live.[1] Anger is a common emotion at support groups, as our friends Diane and Roger discovered when they lost their eighteen-year-old daughter to cancer a few years before David died. One woman told Diane, "Anger is the only thing that keeps me going."

It's only natural to be vulnerable and upset when others show little empathy or concern for our situations. Two people who were lifelong friends practically ignored me at David's funeral and soon afterward. When I expressed my anger about this to my sister-in-law, she promptly told me they probably did not know what to say and advised me to "forgive and forget." End of story. Oh, that it could be that easy! I knew she was right, but I was not quite ready to forgive at that point.

Why did Jesus talk of forgiving others in the prayer that many of us pray every Sunday? Maybe for "us" as much as for "them." Anger has its limitations. Holding on to it is an unhealthy way to live. Lewis Smedes, author of *Forgive and Forget: Healing the Hurts We Don't Deserve,* states we have three choices for handling unfair pain:

1. You can try to deny it and make believe it never happened.
2. You can try to get even, but, as Smedes says, "getting even is a loser's game."
3. You can forgive, which is hardest by far, but it's the only healthy way to cope with the situation.[2]

Forgiveness is a difficult concept and a demanding process, as I am reminded by these notes scribbled down years ago during a sermon on the subject:

> The cost of forgiveness is giving up the right to get even. Forgiveness is giving up resentment of a person or giving up the claim to requital. We have heard it said and probably have also said ourselves, I can forgive but I can't forget. Forgiveness does not mean that sad memories and hurt feelings will not reoccur. Even though forgiveness may heal the lingering pain of the past, we may still feel anger and hurt when memories are triggered—possibly by similar events of the mishap or events that connect you to your loss. Refusing to forgive gives another person control over you.
>
> Forgiving does not mean forgetting. Forgetting is impossible for many people who have suffered great loss.
>
> To forgive does not mean not wanting justice to prevail. People cannot be given license to do what will hurt another human being. Forgiveness does not free the wrongdoer of guilt or erase the natural consequences of the wrong done. Forgiving is trusting God to be God rather than taking the responsibility of righting all wrongs into our own hands.[3]

Forgiveness doesn't mean excusing another's actions, Smedes says, but making an effort to understand them.[4] In his book, Jerry Sittser makes a clear distinction between unforgiveness and healthy response to loss. Anger and grief are both natural responses to loss. The pursuit of justice shows a belief in the moral order of the universe.

Forgiveness is often the most difficult when justice is not served, e.g., when abusive parents continue to terrorize their children and when rapists are not convicted. Though often justice does prevail and wrongdoers are punished, when victims realize that the punishment does not compensate for their loss, sometimes they want more than justice. They want revenge.

When we read the newspapers, we see examples of the devastation caused by revenge. This destruction can take place on a large scale, as we see in Northern Ireland or in the Middle East. On a smaller scale, we see it in gang warfare and family feuds. Because the pain often does not go away, revenge can become endless.[5]

Marilyn Heavilin lost three sons before adulthood; she understands the deep pain of loss. She gives a practical approach to forgiveness, noting that forgiveness does not have a timetable. Quick forgiveness may possibly be sincere, but until a person has an understanding of the loss incurred, the act of forgiving may not be genuine.

Heavilin offers three doable steps in your path to forgiving: First, be willing to forgive. This allows the process to begin. Second, admit your pain and anger; allow the feelings to come out in a way that is harmless to yourself and others, maybe through journalizing or punching a pillow. Finally, identify the offenders you want to forgive.[6]

Heavilin adds another important step—accept the results even if they are not what you desire. Your act of forgiving can free your heart from resentment and hate, but it may not necessarily change the behavior of the person you forgive.[7]

At some point, many of us realize that the one we need to forgive is God. We feel that He has let us down. We're angry at Him. After all, with all His power and wisdom, taking care of David shouldn't have been very hard.

I am not saying that God needs forgiveness. I believe that God is sovereign.

Who is the only One that does not need forgiveness? God.

Who forgives the most? God.

Whom does God desire us to be like? His Son, Jesus.

Are we capable of that? No.

Can we, with His help? If we want to.

Will we be happier if we do? Yes.

Will this eliminate all bad feelings? That probably depends on time and the severity of our hurt. It would seem that God would not ask us to do what is impossible.

When Pastor Dan preached about forgiveness one Sunday, he pointed out that not forgiving people is one way of showing we think their sins are greater than ours. He concluded with the statement "When I look at you, I am looking at a group of sinners." I responded with a loud "AMEN!"

As we left worship service, Pastor Dan told the person ahead of me in line that he had heard his "Amen." I countered, "That was me." My response surprised me more than him! Please take this on faith: I have never before spontaneously replied out loud to a sermon; it is not my style or personality. But his statement hit a chord in my heart. I know I am a sinner. I make mistakes and am quite capable of selfishness.

Forgiving ourselves is often the most difficult step. Many of us think and say negative things about ourselves that we would never say to another. Why is it so hard to live in the confidence that we are who we are, not what we should be? Who are we? Complex people made in the image of God, who dearly loved us and sacrificed His Son so that we might be forgiven.

Many of us have sung the song "Just a Closer Walk with Thee." A close relationship with God requires honesty. Expressing your true feelings to God gives you closer fellowship with Him. By acknowledging your pain and confusion, you are able to get back on speaking terms with God.

Since I was a young adult, I have turned to the Bible for comfort, inspiration, and direction. One thing I didn't appreciate: The standards are very high. I know I do not measure up. If we were able to measure up, God would not have had to sacrifice His Son, the only person who did measure up. Since I don't live up to the standards set forth in the Bible, do I have the right to expect others to live up to my standards? That includes the two friends I mentioned who hurt me by not acknowledging my grief. Gradually I was able to accept that possibly they were not able to express or feel empathy.

I noticed in my reading that some have dealt with injured feelings by confronting those who hurt them. Though tempted,

I recalled friends and acquaintance who went through tough times. Though my heart ached for them, I allowed my own problems and uncertainty of what to say or do to prevent me from saying or doing what I could to ease their pain. God forgives me for my shortcomings and asks me to forgive others.

Which brings us back to Jesus, who offered Himself to fill the gap between what He did (lived a sinless life) and was, and what we do and are.

Pastor Dan pointed out in a recent sermon that we often live in defeat because we forget who we are. We need to live what has been given us. Because we are forgiven, we do not need to live with a sense of failure.

Didn't every Old Testament "hero" occasionally mess up big-time? When we realize we are forgiven, we can look at people differently. We are freed to love each other. Even those who disappoint us and hurt us. The goal is to choose not to live in our failures and other people's failures, but choose to live in forgiveness. That doesn't mean we won't take back our grudge the next day, but we can keep working on it.

Jesus offers the gift of forgiveness and grace. Isn't this gift *much more* amazing than all the miracles He did?

To forgive is to set a prisoner free
and discover that the prisoner was you.
Lewis B. Smedes

Forgiveness is the final form of love.
Reinhold Niebuhr

It is always the case that when the Christian looks back,
he is looking at the forgiveness of sins.
Karl Barth

Say Goodbye to Regrets

And the God of all grace who called you
to his eternal glory in Christ,
after you have suffered a little while,

will himself restore you and make you
strong, firm, and steadfast.
-1 Peter 5:10 NIV

I believe the cause of David's death was bipolar; however, it was bipolar plus the circumstances of his life. The cards he was dealt were all aggravated by a serious and painful disease.

During the months after David's death, my mind buzzed with a litany of "if onlys." If only I had suggested he give himself a break for at least a month after his studies as many of his colleagues did before jumping into working as a lawyer. If only I had fought the stay of commitment. If only I had called more. If only I had listened more and talked less. If only I could have remained serene.

After discussion with a counselor a few times and sharing with several friends and my sisters and praying and talking to God about it, I concluded that I was a loving and conscientious mother dealing with a horrible illness.

I finally decided it is a little arrogant to think I could hold the power of life and death over another person. God had given me the privilege of raising a family, but that privilege carried no guarantees.

Jerry Sittser has a wonderful statement in his book *A Grace Disguised*: "We cannot change the situation, but we can allow the situation to change us."[8] The best way to honor David and show my love to him is to live again with thankfulness to God for having him as my son for thirty-three years and for the family members, relatives, and friends I cherish.

I also learned something very simple yet very profound: things happen in life that even mothers cannot prevent or fix.

But the Jerusalem that is above is free,
and she is our mother. For it is written:
"Be glad, O barren woman who bears no children;
Break forth and cry aloud, you who have no labor pains;
Because more are the children of the desolate woman
Than of her who has a husband."
—Galatians 4:26-27 NIV

CHAPTER 9

One Day at a Time Is Too Much

I haven't a clue as to how my story will end. But that's all right.
When you set out on a journey and night covers the road,
you don't concludethat the road has vanished.
And how else could we discover the stars?[1]

—Unknown

Do you remember the time when you felt most loved? For me it was the week of David's death. Wrapped in the care of others, I had no way to know the void that would follow. Grief is an unknown place until you reach it.

Usually when we embark on a trip, we know the destination and the time that will be involved. I was now on a journey I hadn't planned. With the grief journey, there is no timetable. Nor is there a way to cancel the trip.

This chapter is about what I learned on my grief voyage—things that helped me and might help you. I discovered, you see, that while grief is universal, every response to grief is individual, unique.

I also discovered that grief is not the enemy. Grieving is necessary. We don't burn out because we don't care, but because we don't grieve. Our capacity to love is one of the ways we are made in the image of God. And our grief provides hard evidence of how deeply we have loved.

*   *   *

Two weeks after David's death, needing routine, I returned to my part-time job at a small business. For two years thereafter, the only time I felt almost "normal" was when I was at work.

My coworkers were supportive, but still, for the first few weeks I could not figure out what other people were so happy about. Everywhere I went, to the store, down the sidewalk, other people seemed cheerful. Their worlds were producing happiness, while my own was producing only somberness.

Though not a hermit by nature, I did not want to see friends and acquaintances at grocery stores. They'd ask me how I was doing. Usually I said fine or OK, as expected. How could I explain to them how I felt? Would they even want to hear? I was afraid they would act like nothing had happened, which would make me wonder if they knew or cared about what happened to our family.

Longing to hear David's voice on the answering machine, I called his phone number several times, but his message had been removed. Many more times in the following weeks, I dialed his number only to hear the voices of strangers.

Confusion reigned. There seemed to be a fog between the world and me. Compared to my pain, the world was very uninteresting. My mind and body were so caught up in my grief that they felt numb. I could not tell—and did not want to know—when others were hurting.

I was unable to tell people how I felt either. Talking about my loss made me feel self-absorbed. I said to my sisters, "I don't understand it, I have gotten so selfish." (Eventually the counselor I visited a few times helped me understand that it is not selfish to ask for help when it is needed, that selfishness is when we don't reciprocate when we can.)

My body responded to the loss. I had chronic trouble sleeping, anxiety, and low energy. I woke up in the middle of the night and could not go back to sleep. During the day I was tired all the time.

Even driving a car was difficult at times. Two or three weeks after the funeral I drove to my sister's house—a place I had driven to countless times. Halfway there I looked around, confused. Where was I? I had taken wrong turns. I backtracked, got my bearings. Eventually I got there. It occurred to me to be embarrassed, but I decided not to be. I was grieving. I rang the doorbell, walked in the door, and silently congratulated myself that I got there at all. This experience gave me even more compassion for every person with a mental illness for whom these symptoms are routine and a lifetime challenge.

David died three months before my high school reunion. I told John I no longer wanted to attend. He said, "Yes, you do." Several friends encouraged me to go. So I went, and I was glad I did.

There is a difference between feeling good and feeling good about feeling good, however, as I discovered eight months after David's death. John and I were invited to a lovely Christmas party with many of our favorite things—scrumptious food, interesting guests, stimulating conversation, and a bus ride to a theater where we enjoyed wonderful music. It was a perfect night. As we rode the bus back to our car, I looked out the window at the beautiful skyline and lights. I tried to appreciate everything, but I felt completely empty as I thought of how much David would have enjoyed these things. Guilt and sadness robbed me of any joy.

*   *   *

When we honestly ask ourselves which persons in our lives
mean the most to us, we often find that it is those who,
instead of giving much advice, solutions, or cures,
have chosen rather to share our pain and
touch our wounds with a gentle and tender hand.
The friend who can be silent with us
in a moment of despair or confusion,
who can stay with us in an hour of grief and bereavement,
who can tolerate not-knowing, not-curing, not-healing
and face with us the reality of our powerlessness,
that is the friend who cares.2
—Henri Nouwen

My friend Mary Leean, who had lost a child in a tragic horse accident, told me to never try stopping the tears. Crying had never come easy for me, but I found that following her advice was as natural as breathing. For many months, my days began with a "morning cry" in the garden, an essential part of getting up and getting going.

After a while, my need to cry diminished, and the morning cry ended. Then depression set in. I hurt too much to cry. My thoughts turned constantly to the days before mental illness invaded our family. I yearned for the time when there were more good days than bad ones.

Thank God, my husband and I grieved differently. John was wonderful. He harvested the crops, got meals when I forgot to, helped me plant our flowers, patted my shoulder, and told me I would be feeling better soon. His calm spirit brought a sense of strength and normalcy to our lives. Yet I knew he was grieving too.

A husband and wife are rarely at the same place in their grieving. They have different kinds of investments with the child they lost and different ways and times of working through their grief. When one is up, the other may be down.

Depression, guilt, and inability to get pleasure from simple things in life can be harmful to marriage. It is always easy for one or both partners to blame the other for their unhappiness. Lightheartedness and laughter on the part of one may be hurtful to the spouse who is not ready for fun. A mother may be unable to stop talking about the death of her child for months; the father, though suffering equally, may internalize his feelings. Dr. Robert R. Thompson states, "Statistics show that fully 80 percent of marriages will have some serious disruption, either divorce or separation, after the loss of a child. On a scale of stressful life events, the death of a child is highest on the scale."[3]

I remember visiting a couple after they lost a child in a tragic accident. My heart went out to the father, knowing that men feel grief the same as women but often find it harder to cry than women. It's difficult for me to understand how people can heal from a tragedy such as losing a child without being emotional, but I also know that those who do not express their feelings openly often have their own way of working through the grief process, as I witnessed with my own husband.

In a small country church many years earlier, John and I spoke our wedding vows with joy and commitment. "For richer or poorer, in sickness and health, in good times and bad." At the time we had no way to know what these beautiful words truly meant. Now we do.

If I were to choose one word that explains what enabled us to keep our marriage strong, it would be *acceptance*. Acceptance that we are two different people who grieve differently. That acceptance was a gift from God. It takes a lot of effort to apply the gift in the marital relationship, but it is possible through His grace.

The Myths of Grief, the Tasks of Mourning

"Grief," says psychotherapist Richard Obershaw, "is a process whereby we: (1) identify the fullness of a loss we've incurred; (2) identify the feelings that result from the loss; and (3) begin to re-identify who we are now, after that loss."[4]

We have a number of myths about grief, myths that raise impossible expectations and keep grievers from telling others their true feelings, keep them from telling who they really are. Obershaw lists some of these myths in his book *Cry Until You Laugh.* I've added my thoughts on each.

1. "Time will heal." Time does not heal; hard work brings healing. Birth and death are both hard work. There is labor before birth and labor after death or other painful loss.
2. "You'll get over it." You will never get over it. You are not the same person you were before your loss. If tears flow many years after the death of a loved one, you are not crazy. That grief is a result of genuine love.
3. "This is just a stage you're going through." The problem with this is you may use stages as events you expect to happen which you have no control over. Grief is a process of working through the feelings that result from your loss.

4. "True believers don't cry." The shortest verse of the Bible is "Jesus wept." Jesus was human and wanted and needed to express the grief within Him.
5. "Anticipated grief is easier to handle." I heard a speaker whose young son died after years of leukemia. He certainly had time to be prepared, but his grief was intense and lasted many, many years.
6. "All death means loss." If the relationship was cruel or abusive, the survivor may have feelings of relief and joy.
7. "All gain means happiness." Even the birth of a child can bring some loss, like privacy and freedom.
8. "Survivors only grieve for the loss of the dead." As a mother, I grieved for my whole family, the brother and lifelong true friend my sons lost, the son my husband lost.[5]

Every person has his own pace and way of coping with grief. We who grieve are not powerless. We need to work to remind others about these myths—to reduce our own and others' needless suffering.

Obershaw talks about the "tasks of mourning." I refer to them instead as "hard labor," comparable to the labor of giving birth—except that the labor of grieving is harder and takes much longer.

The first task is accepting the reality of our loss. There will be no reunion in this life. Talking about and remembering the death helps us to accept the reality.

The second task is to experience the pain of our grief. There are many unhealthy, temporary ways to avoid pain, but they only prolong the grieving process. Two ways to avoid the pain of loss are to either idealize the dead or to make a devil out of the deceased.

Sometimes people move, thinking that a different location will have fewer things to remind them of their loss. However, we take our pain with us. It is vital that we accept the hard work of experiencing the fullness of the pain of our loss and important that we help others accept that task.

The third task of mourning is to adjust to our new world. Things are not the same. We need to recognize our loss and how our lives have changed because of it and prepare to deal with this new world we must face.[6]

The fourth task is probably the hardest—taking the emotional energy we have invested into the person or object we lost and reinvesting it into someone or something else. "But, the reality is, all relationships will end. All jobs will end. All health will end. All life will end."[7] Failing to realize this unpleasant fact may prevent us from appreciating the reality of our health, our jobs, our relationships, our lives. I realize now I never truly understood and appreciated David and his life until he died. After his death I learned things about him I might never have learned if he had outlived me.

After working through these stages, we should, at some point, show some signs of identifying ourselves in a different way. The first sign is ability to talk out loud about the loss. Being able to talk about the full personality of the loss or of the person who died is another sign. Your loved one is a "wonderful man" rather than "perfect." A third sign is the ability to feel good about feeling good.[8]

Myths of grief can raise unrealistic expectations. Even before reading the myths Obershaw listed in his book, I had discovered on my own journey that the myths may be popular, but they certainly weren't working for me. We've all heard the saying "The truth hurts." The truth does hurt in the short run, but in the long run it helps us face reality and avoid more pain and confusion.

Walking Back to Life: Some Paths

As you walk back to life, you need to take tiny steps. People talk about taking things "one day at a time," but in my experience even "one day at a time" is too hard when you're experiencing deep grief or loss.

The fall after David died, Mother Nature painted our peas and our corn and soybean fields green, bronze, and golden brown right on schedule. Beauty and fruitful growth abounded outside our farm home. Trees turned to bright orange, red, bronze, and yellow, the last hurrah before they shed their leaves.

My soul remained gray and dull. I got up in the morning. What should I do? What was the point of doing it? I sought company.

Then I wondered, was it wrong to burden others with my sorrow? Should I try to get through this by myself? The answers were NO! and NO! We all need people we trust, friends who not only laugh with us but also cry with us. If you sense the gift of empathy in another, seek that person out. Support groups can help us realize that we are never alone in our grief. Counselors are also important. Clergy are another good choice. Not all are trained in counseling, but you can always ask your pastor if there is anyone in the congregation who might have an understanding of your sorrow and who could help you over the rough hurdles of pain.

It's more healing to cry with someone than to cry alone. My sisters, Bernie and Sharon, shared my tears. It was comforting too when my friend Pat Hanson said, "You know, none of us understand what you and John are going through," and so helpful to be reminded I should not expect others to understand my pain when they hadn't been there yet.

*   *   *

When I decided to be more serious about my faith in Christ, I went through Bible study booklets with titles containing words like *prayer, confessing sin, forgiving,* etc. I felt after each book that I had made some progress. The problem was that I started with the assumption that each study would move me a little bit farther in the maturation process. Not true. These were steps that needed to be repeated again and again. Now, decades later, I still don't feel "advanced."

The same applies to grieving. The ten stages of grief that Granger Westberg lists in *Good Grief* are helpful in showing us the universality of our grief and in assuring us we are not going crazy. It is easy to read them and assume that after each stage you "advance" to the next until you arrive. Not true. Although most grievers experience most or all of these stages, Westberg cautions, not every person goes through *all* the stages and not necessarily in this order:

1. We are in a state of shock. This may last from a few minutes, to a few hours, to a few days, to several weeks. If prolonged, seek professional help. In the funeral home, the almost radiant wife or mother may be experiencing the anesthesia that shock gives to help her along to the next stage of grief.
2. We express emotion. These reactions help you survive during difficult times. Tears are healing, so don't try to stop them.
3. We feel depressed and very lonely. In this stage we wonder if God cares and are sure that no one has ever grieved as we have. We are right! We all grieve in different ways.
4. We may experience physical symptoms of distress. This may include heart palpitations, stomach pains, chest pains, or dizziness.
5. We may become panicky. Our work shows we are not producing the quantity and quality of work we are capable of. It is very hard to concentrate.
6. We feel a sense of guilt about the loss. At this stage, the person who believes in the divine gift of forgiveness and acceptance will be able to admit guilt if appropriate and move on to forgiveness.
7. We are filled with anger and resentment. These emotions are part of being human, but they can also be very harmful. They are a normal part of the grief process but need to be wrestled with and overcome by the grace of God. During this stage we are critical of everyone and anyone related to our loss. I remember, for instance, being annoyed at the remark of a friend who visited the day before the funeral. She said, "God works in mysterious ways His wonders to perform." I didn't want to understand the mysterious ways of God. I just wanted David back. I wanted to hear his terrific laugh, smell his aftershave, feel his days' growth of whiskers as I brushed my face against him and gave him a hug, spar with him on a lively political or religious debate. In time I learned that, although people often say insensitive things during this

hard journey of ours, we need to realize that it is simply their way of reaching out.

8. We resist returning to our normal activities. Everyone else is turning to other activities and conversation. We feel that they do not understand how great our loss was. Our customs and way of life make it difficult to grieve in front of other people, so we grieve within ourselves. People often avoid talking about the deceased, thinking it may hurt the grieving person. (*I assure you* that we long to talk about the deceased loved one.)

9. Gradually hope comes through.

10. We struggle to affirm reality. This does not mean we are our old selves again. We are different people. We are either stronger or weaker.[9]

A Question and Test of Faith

At a "Growth Through Loss" session in Eagan, Minnesota, the speaker, Mitch, described his grief after the painful death of his son nearly two decades earlier. He said we should grieve the way we want to grieve. Mitch said the amount of your grief will be proportional to the amount of your love. If you loved hard, you will grieve hard. He cautioned that the death of a child is a lifelong journey and encouraged us to take the risk to be as good as we can be. He considered belief in a higher power necessary in this journey.

> Love's as hard as nails
> Love is Nails:
> Blunt, thick, hammered through
> The medial nerve of One
> Who, having made us, knew
> The thing He had done,
> Seeing (with all that is)
> Our cross and his.
> —C. S. Lewis

Grief can strain marriages. It can also strain faith. One friend told me that after her son died, God hid Himself from her. I also wondered where God was in all this confusion. Just when I needed Him most, He seemed so very distant.

I wanted to let God love me, but I was finding it hard to believe He loved anyone, judging by what He had allowed to happen to my family. Still I clung to and prayed the Psalms. For many months they brought no release from pain, but they did get me through the day. In my heart I knew God loved me in my sorrow, in my anger, in my doubts. Jesus prayed that His cup of pain and death and suffering be removed. God loved His Son and He loved us. He sacrificed His son to suffer for our redemption.

Believing in everlasting life does not lessen the need for grieving. Some claim that if you believe in everlasting life, it should be a time of rejoicing. When a person dies after a long and fruitful life, we can rejoice in his homecoming and still miss his presence in our life. When David died so unexpectedly, it was a tragedy. It was not possible for us to make his death a celebration.

How we work through our grief is not as important as the task itself. Through reading, counseling, friends, grief groups, or prayer, we can gather the strength and support we will need to work through our loss.

Church denomination or names cannot define us. May this quotation from Corinne Chilstrom's book, *Andrew, You Died Too Soon,* give you comfort if you are grieving:

> Luther says not to sit and brood, but "lift your eyes . . . take a Psalm . . . and pour out your trouble with tears before God, lamenting and calling upon him . . ." He wills that you should be too weak to bear and overcome such trouble, in order that you may learn to find strength in Him, and that He may be praised through His strength in you. Behold, this is how Christians are made![10]

Nothing prepared me for losing my son. I had gone through loss many times. Our dogs and cats who were "members of the family" and the loss of each was sad. My grandparents when

I was very young. My father due to a heart attack when I was thirteen. He loved his family, was full of life and passionate about fishing. My mother died of a stroke when I was twenty-four.

My parents were young, but I was young enough to consider them "old." My life was endlessly before me. None of these losses prepared me in any way for the loss of David. David, at age thirty-three, seemed so very young.

Healing was not to be given here on earth. Maybe the illness David had will enable to us to experience more joy later. One thing I know is that David is now healed. He is free. Bipolar, you won a few battles, but God has won the war.

The children of your servants will live in your presence;
their descendants will be established before you.
—Ps. 102:28 NIV

*   *   *

Grieve not as those who have no hope.
—1 Thessalonians 4:13 NIV

Stages of Grief

Granger Westberg in *Good Grief* suggests that in the above eight words of scripture, we insert a comma, "Grieve, not as those who have not hope," and then add, "but for goodness' sakes grieve when you have something worth grieving about!"[11]

Most people avoid grief, yet grief is necessary. A loss is a wound, and grieving is the healing process to mend that wound. Many would like to ignore suffering. Yet becoming numb to suffering will not make us happy. The part in us that feels suffering is the same part that feels joy.

Some believe that spiritually mature people do not need to grieve. Their faith will get them through their loss. Yet the scriptures, both Old and New Testament, show grief as a normal part of life. Chapter 13 of 2 Samuel tells of the heartache King David suffered from turmoil in his family. King David, known as a man after God's own heart, mourned for his son Amnon every day after his death. It took him three years to be consoled. Did King David's mourning make him less spiritual?

I know I needed to grieve. My poem "Birth and Death of a Dream" flowed out of my birth and death experience. Labor was needed to deliver life. The labor of grief was needed to cope with loss through death.

Dr. Erich Lindermann, professor of psychiatry at Harvard, cited by Westberg, points out five things he saw in acute grief: "(1) somatic distress, (2) preoccupation with the image of the deceased, (3) guilt, (4) hostile reactions, and (5) loss of patterns of conduct." Lindermann's studies found that "parishioners who faced up to their loss by wrestling openly and honestly with the problem came through the grieving experience stronger, deeper, and better able to help others with their grieving."[12]

This wrestling may cause grievers to reevaluate and question their faith. Even if this gives birth to doubts, if a relationship with God through regular worship and fellowship with church members who really care about you is maintained, the struggle can deepen your faith and produce growth.[13]

We cannot control our grief, but we can control some things:

1. Eating three meals a day
2. Maintaining social contact when you really don't feel like it
3. Exercising
4. Continuing to nourish your spiritual values and practices
5. Even when—especially when—you don't feel like doing them, the above four will give you some control when everything else seems out of control. Flesh and blood people are needed in our grief journey.

We also need a power higher than ourselves. The higher power can be sought through regular worship. Here are some notes I took from one of Pastor Dan Horn's sermons at Christ United Church of Cannon Falls, Minnesota, which gave me—and can give you—comfort:

> All of us go through tough times. Granted some trials
> are more soul wrenching than others. Some trials are

temporary, some are chronic, a way of life. Whichever ship we are on, our challenge is the same: "Hang on to God in the midst of the storm." He will be there.

James 1 is one of those paradoxical "turn the wisdom of the world upside down" passages. First we are told to count it joy when we have many trials, then advised to rejoice if we are poor because we have God. We are told *not* to rejoice in our wealth because it is temporary. Either way the important thing is to hang on to God. How are we supposed to apply this? When we are poor, do we trust Him as if we had everything? When we are rich, do we trust Him as if we had nothing? God calls us to a life of dependence on the Father.

There is a difference between God's reality and the world's reality. Our life may seem out of control, but God is in control.

Your reaction to the notes above might be similar to mine when my nurse told me the day after my knee revision to get out of bed and walk to the bathroom. "You're kidding, of course!" So consider this real-life example. I remember reading in *World Vision* magazine about a destitute woman who had known poverty, war, and hardship all her life. She did not have shelter from the elements or enough to eat. She had been given a simple rag by a neighbor. When she was interviewed by a reporter, she said to the reporter, "God is good. Why else would I have this rag that I need?"

She was poor but thankful, poor in things of the world, but rich in God.

*   *   *

Marilyn Heavilin, in her book *When Your Dreams Die,* states in the early stages of grief, since this world seems too painful, many yearn for the second coming of Christ. It is not uncommon in the early stages of grief to spend a lot of time thinking about heaven. "What do they do there? Are they aware of us?"[14]

In the middle stages of grief, the pain subsides for brief moments periodically. The waves of grief still come, but they are less frequent and do not last as long. You have become more fully aware of the injustice of your situation. Some are obsessed with the desire to change the wrongs of the world. Grievers can become single-minded in their mission and may neglect everything and everyone else around them. Holidays have often become easier by not being tied to traditions. Birthdays, death days, and anniversaries are still painful.

In the later stages of grief you feel more normal and comfortable. You would like to go back, but you accept this new normal as second best. The waves of grief become infrequent, but you still think of your loss fairly often. Holidays become tolerable, some you even look forward to. Birthdays, death days, and anniversaries will never be forgotten, but their impact lessens. You long for life to be thrilling again, but you discover the excitement of life is dulled because of your trauma. You feel you have been robbed of your innocence.[15]

Even at the last stage, grief is not fully resolved for everyone. John and I recently visited with an old friend. We reminisced about his son who had died seventeen years earlier. He was calmly talking about his son's death and suddenly became overcome with tears. John and I silently grieved with him. We understood.

People of faith grieve deeply and go through the same stages. All wrestle with their faith during grief, but those with a mature faith seem to wrestle more effectively because of their conviction that God is still with them. They do not need to face the future alone. Many develop a deeper faith in God because of their grief. They will be stronger and better able to help others who face similar tragedies.

This inner strength, Westberg says, grows out of their belief that their relationship with God is one thing that can never be taken away from them. They may not understand why God allowed the pain, but they believe He truly cares. Even though life may never be the same again, they realize that not everything has been taken away. There is much in life that can be affirmed as good. No matter how great a loss or how deep the pain, one thing they will always have—their relationship with a loving God! Nobody wants grief because grief is painful, but grief can be good grief.[16]

Westberg concludes, "It is not right that people should try to carry on grief work alone. People through the centuries have found new and unexpected strength in the words, 'I am with you always.' So we say, 'Grieve—not as those who have no hope,' but please, when you have something to grieve about, go ahead and grieve."[17]

> Those who bear the mark of pain
> are never really free;
> They owe a debt to the ones
> who still suffer.
> —Anonymous

Can We Cancel Christmas This Year?

For many, holidays, anniversaries, birthdays, and death days are intolerable during early stages of grief. The empty chair and black hole in your soul are ever present. Your only goal is to live through them.

During the first year after David's death, I went to a grief meeting, numbly listening while the speaker cheerfully told of how she celebrated Christmas after the death of her elderly father who had lived a long and fulfilling life. My mind glazed over as she described the ornaments she made that illustrated things that were meaningful to her father and his life instead of buying the usual Christmas wreath.

What was she talking about? Where would I get the energy to make an elaborate wreath in memory of David? It would be amazing if I could find the energy to give minimal gifts with a check attached, go to church, and cook a simple meal.

Several days later I sat in the whirlpool after swimming at the Northfield Senior Center listening to the lady with me pleasantly chat about her plans for gifts, baking, seeing family, and other happy events. Struggling to listen, I softly said, "I wish I could cancel Christmas this year." If she heard, she did not acknowledge my comment, for she continued with her dialog of Christmas plans.

The thought of the annual spate of Christmas letters made my stomach churn. I wanted to be spared the ghastly details of happiness and success of every other family around me as I wallowed in my pain and loneliness. Even though I was definitely not in the mood, Matt convinced me to write a Christmas letter. It is excerpted below:

2005 CHRISTMAS GREETINGS!!
For unto us a child is born, to us a Child is given. Isa. 9:6

Dear Friends,

Let me share a conversation on Thanksgiving Day this year:

Grandniece Ellie Ann (age 3): "Did you know that Jesus was once a baby?"

Me (Pat): "Yes, I did. How long ago was He born?"

Ellie Ann, seriously pondering my question: "A *long* time ago."

Adam (age 6), ready to help his sister: "About 500 years ago."

With our advantage of age over Ellie and Adam, we can say Jesus was born about 2000 years ago, and so we celebrate this Christmas season.

I told Matt that I didn't feel like sending a Christmas letter this year. His reply: "If ever there was a year you should write one, it's this year. A few of our friends have probably not heard of David's death."

In most of my Christmas letters I have acknowledged and grieved with friends for whom Christmas may be a difficult time to celebrate for many reasons—loss of health, a loved one, a problem that eludes solution. This Christmas I grieve myself—for unto us (my family) a son, a brother, a lifelong friend was given, but on April 19, David was taken . . .

David was a wonderful gift, and our loss is great, but there is much we have not lost. Relationships and memories are eternal. When my friend Anita May and I cried together, I pointed out that David died at age 33—my mother's age when I was born. Anita responded, "The age that Jesus died." That is why a Child was given—to bring us to an eternal relationship with God. We marvel that God loved us *all* so much He was willing to give His *only* begotten Son!

I was determined to be "cheerful" for John's sake. It didn't work. Keeping up appearances wasn't working. I wasn't much fun to be around. I was one wretched (or bitchy) woman. Finally, John said, "Enough!" So I acknowledged my sadness and frustration to John. And yes, we made up.

It was too cold to go out to my garden, so I had a lengthy personal devotion until my heart was finally quiet. Then I looked at many of the Christmas cards I had received the previous year that I saved as a reminder of our friendships. After some quiet time, here was my conclusion of the point of Christmas:

I ask myself,
WHO IS THIS JESUS?
What is He to me?
What do I want Him to be?
Then, I reaffirm,
Who He has been,
What He has been,
Who He can be,
If I let Him.
JESUS,
helpless, crying BABY,
gentle GUIDE,
loyal FRIEND,
suffering SAVIOUR,
returning, victorious KING
wiping away all our TEARS.
And so may we all ask,
WHO IS THIS JESUS?
What is He to me?
What do I want Him to be?

—Pat Day

*   *   *

Now the dwelling of God is with men, and He will live with them.
They will be his people, and God himself will be
with them and be their God.
He will wipe every tear from their eyes.
There will be no more death or mourning or crying or pain,
for the old order of things has passed away.
—Revelation 21:3-4 NIV

Count Your Losses, Name Them One By One

Paul V. Johnson, a specialist in grief and loss and professor at Bethel University, was the speaker at a "Grief and Loss" talk given at Northfield Hospital about a year after David's death. He distributed a handout listing painful losses.

- We are traumatized by the death of a loved one or close friend.
- We are hurt when a profound disappointment comes our way.
- We face the fracturing of a cherished relationship or endure conflict among people we love.
- We see our hopes and dreams for our work put on hold.
- We are under immense stress and strain.
- We feel problems pile up.
- We experience health problems, pain, or life-threatening illness.

Looking over the bulleted list above, it struck me for the first time that when David suffered his first bipolar attack one week before his wedding, he suffered all but one of the above losses. I did not recognize the extent of his loss at that time. How could I? I knew nothing about bipolar, and neither the doctor nor I knew the severity of his illness. That would take years to discover and process. John and I also suffered many of the above losses when David was diagnosed with bipolar.

Johnson gave three questions a grieving person should ask himself:[18]

1. What have I lost?
2. What have I left?
3. What may still be possible for me? One possibility is what you can do in honor of your loved one who died.

Johnson said to allow ten blank pages to answer the first question, "What have I lost?" He said that five years from now we should have moved on from counting our losses and be more focused on what we still have left.

This does not mean the grief has gone. The only way to lose our grief is to lose our memories, and we don't want to do that. "Letting go" is a misnomer. You never let go of their love, their spirit; you let go of what won't be, the dream you lost, and look at what you still have. We need to come to the point where we can live in a new form.

The best advice I found for surviving a painful loss is to try to find gratitude in your heart for what has been. The words of Dag Hammarskjöld in his book *Markings* have inspired many: "For all that has been, Thanks! For all that will be, yes."

This gratitude will come very slowly, so look hard and patiently for it. First, honor and experience the tears and ache in your heart. No matter how much it hurts, name your losses. Pour out your heart to God. Cling to Him in pain and love.

Quilt of Holes

As I faced my Maker at the last judgment, I knelt before the Lord along with all the other souls. Before each of us laid our lives like the squares of a quilt in many piles, an angel sat before each of us sewing our quilt squares together into a tapestry that is our life.

But as my angel took each piece of cloth off the pile, I noticed how ragged and empty each of my squares was. They were filled with giant holes. Each square was labeled with a part of my life that had been difficult, the challenges and temptations I was faced with in everyday life. I saw hardships that I endured, which were the largest holes of all.

I glanced around me. Nobody else had such squares. Other than a tiny hole here and there, the other tapestries were filled with rich color and the bright hues of worldly fortune. I gazed upon my own life and was disheartened.

My angel was sewing the ragged pieces of cloth together, threadbare and empty, like binding air. Finally, the time came when each life was to be displayed, held up to the light, the scrutiny of truth. The others rose, each in turn, holding up their tapestries. So filled their lives had been. My angel looked upon me and nodded for me to rise.

My gaze dropped to the ground in shame. I hadn't had all the earthly fortunes. I had love in my life, and laughter. But there had also been trials of illness, and health, and false accusations that took from me my world, as I knew it. I had to start over many times.

I often struggled with the temptation to quit, only to somehow muster the strength to pick up and begin again. I spent many nights on my knees in prayer, asking for help and guidance in my life. I had often been held up to ridicule, which I endured painfully, each time offering it up to the Father in hopes that I would not melt within my skin beneath the judgmental gaze of those who unfairly judged me. And now, I had to face the truth. My life was what it was, and I had to accept it for what it was. I rose and slowly lifted the combined squares of my life to the light. An awe-filled gasp filled the air. I gazed around at the others who stared at me with wide eyes.

Then, I looked upon the tapestry before me. Light flooded the many holes, creating an image, the face of Christ. Then our Lord stood before me, with warmth and love in His eyes. He said, "Every time you gave over your life to Me, it became My life, My hardships, and My struggles. Each point of light in your life is when you stepped aside and let Me shine through, until there was more of Me than there was of you."

May all our quilts be threadbare and worn, allowing Christ to shine through!

Source: Sent to me over the Internet by a friend

Though you have made me see troubles,
many and bitter, you will restore my life again;
from the depths of the earth you will again bring me up.
You will increase my honor and comfort me once again.
Psalms 71: 20-21, NIV

He will yet fill your mouth with laughter
and your lips with shouts of joy.
Job 8:21, NIV

CHAPTER 10

More Than Survivors: Words Do Help

Laura Sterling lit a candle to brighten her corner of the world. Seeing the grief and suffering of suicide survivors in her area, she rolled up her sleeves and started a LOSS (Loved Ones Surviving Suicide) group, which met monthly in the District One Hospital in Faribault, Minnesota.

We all went to the first meeting broken and wounded. It took several sessions for us to stop crying long enough talk about our loss, but we got there. Though it was painful to see the pain in other survivors' eyes, sharing our tears was healing, and it relieved some of the loneliness. Eventually we were able to start talking.

I share my notes of the message given by Craig Breimhorst, pastor of Christ Lutheran Church in Faribault, Minnesota, which gave us a feeling of peace and hope:

> Because they are afraid of entering into our suffering, people may be hesitant to talk to us. They want us to not suffer so they won't suffer. There are people who don't want to listen because it may cause them pain. When you are willing to listen and feel others' suffering, you are Jesus right then.
>
> Stuffing our feelings can block healing. Anger is natural and can give us a feeling of control, but it is not a healthy way to live. Prolonged anger can make us unable to love anyone else.

However, anger can be a healthy emotion, and there is no need to feel guilty about it. We feel this way because we loved someone. Lazarus was dead when Jesus arrived in his home. Mary and Martha both expressed anger at his death when they said to Jesus, "If you had been here, Lazarus would not have died." We are like Mary and Martha; in our anger, we ask, "God, where were you?" I believe God will do the same for us that he did for Martha and Mary.

Suffering can also be a blessing. We cannot get to the resurrection without the cross. God enters into our crisis to help us and teach us. Jesus took the death of Lazarus and turned it into healing. Jesus was and is the resurrection and the life. By His power, Lazarus arose from the dead. God shines brighter in darkness.

In answer to a question I asked him, Breimhorst said that I or any other mortal can be mistaken as to the situation my son David was in. We have an intellect and will. We have our five senses, our abstract intellect, selective memory. How much reality comes through?

If you had no opportunity to ask for forgiveness before your loved one died, Reverend Breimhorst said he believes in a journey beyond our death. So you can close your eyes and tell the dead person you are sorry.

Breimhorst told us we will remember our loved one better when we partly get over it and suggested we turn to him or her as often as possible in gladness. He encouraged us to praise God because what we praise we enjoy.

In our grief, our ideas of God change. God changes them Himself. The incarnation left previous ideas of the Messiah in ruins. God sees because He loves and loves because He sees. When a loved one dies, we need to continue to love him or her. We also need to love others. Then we can be not only survivors but *more* than survivors!

Everything can change in the blink of an eye.
But don't worry; God never blinks.
—Printed on an e-mail I received

Relationship or Religion?

When I was twenty-three years old, I made a commitment to believe in Christ. Wanting to learn more about God and grow in my relationship, I searched the scriptures, starting with Genesis and reading to the end in my King James Bible. I noticed that God's sovereignty and omnipresence were reflected often in the Bible.

In my grief over David's death, I struggled with many questions:

- Where is God in the midst of our pain?
- Where are my friends when I need them?
- Why are some people's heartfelt prayers answered and not others'?
- Is God random?
- Does suffering have a purpose in itself?
- What is our responsible response to our pain?

The list went on and on.

Finally, I quit asking God and Pastor Dan questions and asked myself a question: "Is my relationship with God dependent on my feelings?"

A story from *Kitchen Table Wisdom* illustrates an important difference between feelings and a relationship:

When she was five years old, Rachel Naomi Remen heard a fire-and-brimstone message delivered by the principal at her public school, who declared that if God did not see you, you would wither and die like an autumn leaf. It terrified her so much that God would blink and she could die that she was unable to sleep.

She shared her fears with her grandfather. He asked her, if she woke up in the night in her room, would she know if her parents had gone and left her alone in the house? When she said she would know, he asked how she would know they were still in the house. Would she see them, hear them, or touch them? Then she knew the answer: she would know without seeing, hearing, or touching that her parents were in the house. She understood. God also knows without seeing, hearing, or touching.

This calmed Remen's fears and helped her achieve an inner knowing that God is there and never changes.[1] Is not her trust similar to the childlike trust in God that Jesus praised?

Remen describes this inner experience with God as "a relationship that's there all the time, even when we're not paying attention to it. Perhaps the Infinite holds us to Itself the same way the earth does. Like gravity, if it ever stopped, we would know it instantly. But it never does."[2]

The Bible asks us to come to God like a little child. Remen had a childlike trust in God. As a child, she knew her parents would never leave her alone. When I was a child, I also knew my parents would never leave me. After they died, though I could not see, touch, or hear them, they remained a part of me. They are alive today in my memory and heart.

Neither can I see the eternal, sovereign God, but I know He will never leave me. The relationship is there all the time because God's presence is always there. I see a bit of His power and sovereignty every day in countless ways: the wonders of the physical world, the comfort He brings to my heart when I quietly seek Him, the many things He has done for me I could never have done for myself. My feelings are changeable and unreliable, but God never changes. He is sovereign, reliable, and omnipresent.

> The man who hates God is not far from the Kingdom.
> It is the spiritually indifferent man who has placed himself
> almost beyond hope.[3]
> —Sherwood Eliot Wirt

Feelings toward God When Your Dream Dies

When you lose someone or something precious to you, despite how much you want to, it is impossible to avoid the feelings of pain. Sometimes the pain is postponed due to shock or an attempt to avoid it, but it is always there. There is no way to ultimately avoid the pain when a dream dies, like the death of a loved one, a loss of health, a divorce canceling hopes for a long and happy relationship, the death of a cherished pet, or a loss of a job you love.

My *CareNotes* pamphlet states that anger is an investment. Anger is not the opposite of love, but often a dimension of it. It is the sign of a "love deeply wounded."[4] After David's death, I felt separated from God for a time. Still I sought Him; in my anger I sought Him.

Harold Kushner's book, *When Bad Things Happen to Good People*, echoed many of my unanswered questions and, yes, my anger at God for allowing so much grief to happen. I loved his honesty and his probing mind.

Kushner describes his friend Helen, who became angry at God when she was diagnosed with multiple sclerosis. Her doctor explained that this degenerative nerve disease would gradually, or maybe quickly, get worse. Finally, she would lose bowel and bladder control, be confined to a wheelchair, and become more of an invalid until death.

As hard as this horrible disease was, it was far harder for her to live with the idea of the randomness and lack of reason for bad things happening to people. There was a sense that God had lost control. Worse yet, she felt guilty for her anger at God.[5] I learned that some people choose to blame themselves for feeling anger. Not knowing this woman, I felt deep empathy. I too felt angry at God. But unlike her, I felt no guilt for my anger.

We cannot separate ourselves from our bodies or our emotions when we pray. Our feelings affect our prayer life. It is easier to "feel" God when we are happy and very hard (maybe impossible) to feel Him during grief. By instinct and through reading of the Psalms, I often prayed my pain.

Several years before David died, John and I visited a church. As we sat in the sanctuary, I was distracted with worries about David. Where was his illness going to take him next? Was I doing enough? Was I doing too much? I wanted my simple "before mental illness" life back.

The worship and praise lifted my spirit some, but I was still deeply worried about David. As first-time visitors, we were given a card to pick up coffee and a donut, and as we stood sipping our coffee, a member of the church approached us and engaged us in conversation. We felt comfortable sharing our concerns with him.

When I shared with him that faith and praise were much easier when you were happy than when you are sad, he agreed 100 percent. His wife had died of cancer the year before. John and I had yet to experience the pain of David's death, but we had suffered enough grief from the losses David suffered from bipolar to sympathize with what C. S. Lewis so eloquently expressed in his book *A Grief Observed*, which he wrote after experiencing the excruciating pain of losing the love of his life. His book on bereavement is moving because of its absolute candor. We can probably all identify with his thoughts and feelings if, or when, we suffer grief:

> Meanwhile, where is God? This is one of the most disquieting symptoms. When you are happy, so happy that you have no sense of needing Him, so happy that you are tempted to feel His claims upon you as an interruption, if you remember yourself and turn to Him with gratitude and praise, you will be—or so it feels—welcomed with open arms. But go to Him when your need is desperate, when all other help is vain, and what do you find? A door slammed in your face, and a sound of bolting and double bolting on the inside. After that, silence . . . Why is He so present a commander in our time of prosperity and so very absent a help in time of trouble?[6]

Be encouraged. At the end of the book Lewis moves back to a world that makes sense and regains a sense of God's presence and love.

When one is going through deep pain, God seems distant. It is not healthy to repress our true feelings. God is not surprised at them. He is strong and wise enough to handle them.

In Psalms God gives us permission to feel angry and discouraged. The Psalms are full of lamentations as well as praise to God. The writers wondered why God was allowing so much pain. They felt free to feel and say anything to God. That is freedom; the Psalms are the perfect example of what freedom of expression means.

Believing in God's sovereignty makes us wonder why He allows tragedies. When I consider His goodness, I believe He doesn't create tragedies, but comforts us through them. My friend Krista Horn shared with me something else that C. S. Lewis wrote: Evil is simply taking something that is good and twisting it. She feels God's goodness can be the reverse of that, taking something evil and turning it into something good. That is one of the greatest definitions of redemption, taking something that has been ruined and bringing life out of it.

> For we do not have a high priest who is unable to sympathize
> with our weaknesses, but we have one who has
> been tempted in every way, just as we are—yet was
> without sin. Let us then approach the throne of grace
> with confidence, so that we may receive mercy and find
> grace to help us in our time of need.
> —Hebrews 4:15-16 NIV

> Be aware of the differences that blind us
> to the unity that binds us.
> —Huston Smith

Wrestling with God

It would be a rare Christian who has not wrestled with God. It would be an even rarer Christian who has not wrestled with God during dark days. When David died, I wrestled with God. My questions and doubts were overwhelming. I believed God heard my prayers, but I wondered how He could answer them in a way that caused such pain to my family. Hadn't I clearly told God my desire that David be able to live with bipolar and be an advocate for this terrible disease? I had shared with God why David could do this: in spite of his illness, he had graduated from the University of Minnesota Law School in three years and passed the bar with flying colors on his first attempt. In addition, he had integrity, logic, and the gift of debate. Certainly he could live with the disease and be an advocate for mental illness! Surely he would never succumb to suicide!

Yet David did commit suicide, and that left me with many serious questions afterward. While I never doubted the existence of God, I did not have the same feeling of trust as I had before. How could I completely trust a God who supposedly had heard my prayers for my son but did not answer them and left him to die? At the same time, I seemed to be surrounded by testimonies of God intervening in others' lives. They filled my ears and made me nauseous. They triggered the question "Why would God intervene for them but not for David?"

But I knew I was in good company. Multitudes of other Christians had had experiences with doubting God. And often they grew closer to Him because of it. It was comforting to know that the existence of my doubts was normal, as normal as the existence of my love for David. It was also comforting to know that God would not spite me for wrestling with Him.

I found great reassurance in the lives of the disciples. All of them had a period of doubting between the time Christ died and the time of His resurrection, and yet Jesus showed Himself to them all in spite of their doubts.

I was particularly encouraged by Thomas, who would not believe the Resurrection until he saw for himself and placed his fingers in the nail holes of Christ's hands and side. Every other disciple had had the opportunity of seeing the risen Christ themselves, but Thomas was not there. He refused to acknowledge their testimony, earning his namesake "doubting Thomas."

He is most well-known for his skepticism at that moment, but Thomas was also noted for his fierce love and devotion to Christ. And this is why I was encouraged by him, not because he doubted, but because he loved the Lord and doubted. When Jesus chose to raise Lazarus from the dead, He had to return to Judea, where the Jews had recently sought to stone Him. Directly after Jesus made that decision, it was Thomas, doubting Thomas, who said, "Let us also go that we may die with him" (John 11:16). His words demonstrated an intense commitment to Christ and belief in His message.

So how could someone so ready to die with Christ be so doubtful that He, the Life Giver, could return to life? How could someone who heard Christ declare, firsthand, that He would die and rise again in three days be so unbelieving of His words? How could someone who had heard the testimony of Mary Magdalene and the other disciples that Christ was alive still be unconvinced that Jesus Christ had indeed risen from the dead? Because even those who have walked most closely with Christ, have seen His face and believed in His message to the point of death, will doubt Him.

After his period of doubt, Thomas went on to establish the church with the other disciples. He devoted himself to prayer with them also (Acts 1:14) and, according to church tradition, was one of the ten of the eleven (all but John) who went on to be martyrs for their faith. So it is possible to not only believe after doubting but grow stronger in faith as well.

My period of wrestling with and doubting God would have been much more disheartening without Thomas's example of hope.

I wrestled with God as to why suicide had entered my family. I doubted whether He had made the right choice to remain silent to my prayers. And I remained confused about David's death for a long time. I'm still confused sometimes. Yet I am able to say that God is good. Because although He did hear my prayers and chose not to intervene, He also wept with us as David died. And He raised our son to eternal life in that moment, which I do not doubt.

> All your sons will be taught by the Lord,
> and great will be your children's peace.
> Isaiah 54:13 NIV

Why? Why Me?

The first question we ask when encountered with pain is usually "Why?" The second question is "Why me?" Isn't it just as logical to ask, "Why did I think I would be spared what so many others have endured?"

During my grief journey I read many books by people who experienced deep grief and learned from it. Our grief was so similar. I felt a bond with each writer.

I would love to have a cup of coffee with Harold S. Kushner, who experienced deep pain and grew in compassion and wisdom. He believed in God and spent most of his life trying to help other people to believe. Yet his personal experience led him to rethink everything he had been taught about God and His ways.

Kushner's daughter Ariel was born when his son Aaron had just passed his third birthday. On the same day as this joyous birth, the local pediatrician visited him and his wife in the hospital and told them Aaron had a condition called "rapid aging" or progeria. The doctor said Aaron would never grow beyond three feet in height, would look like a little old man while he was still a child, would have no hair on his head or body, and would die in his early teens.[7]

Kushner's reaction to this life-changing news was to declare how unfair it was; it didn't make sense. He was devoted to God, his family, and his fellow man, yet his family was now suffering this terrible lot in life. He knew people who were not committed to God yet had large, healthy families. Why was this? It seemed backward. Why would tragedy strike his family?

Despite our knowledge that millions of people suffer pain every day, we tend to not question God until a tragedy hits our home directly.

Kushner's struggle to make sense of random tragedy is shared by nearly all who have felt helpless as they watched someone they love suffer. One example Kushner gave was that of Ron, a young pharmacist shot by a robber stealing drugs and money from his drugstore. The bullet went through his abdomen and into his spinal cord. Ron would never walk again. A friend who believed that everything happens for a purpose pointed out that Ron had always been a confident guy, popular with the girls. He said, "Maybe this is God's way of teaching you a lesson, making you more thoughtful, more sensitive to others." Ron's response to this man was normal: he remembered thinking he would have punched him if he hadn't been confined to a hospital bed.

We have all heard this line of reasoning used in offering comfort. What is the intent? To encourage the sufferer? Ron was not encouraged. Nor would you or I be. Does it echo the desire that bad can be transformed into good, pain into privilege? Or is the intent to defend God? Does God need defending?[8]

The need of the grieving person is physical comfort and compassion that flows from others sharing his pain. A person in despair needs friends who allow him to cry, to be angry.

No one needs "Job's friends," people who make things worse because they are more concerned with their own feelings and needs than those of the hurting person.

The logic which attributes all suffering to God's punishment has far-reaching and painful consequences. One example of those who followed this logic was the people who opposed Edward Jenner's smallpox vaccine. Some of Jenner's strongest opposition came from clergy who believed it interfered with the will of God. Yet without this vaccine, thousands and thousands of people, throughout time, would have suffered and died needlessly.

The problem with this line of reasoning is that it does not acknowledge that we *all* suffer in this world, albeit in different ways and in varying degrees. God did not promise us eternal happiness on earth. While I have heard television evangelists endorse that strong Christian faith will give you prosperity and health, I've also read the apostle Paul, who said that we should not expect health and wealth from the Christian life, but a measure of suffering. He told Timothy, "In fact everyone who wants to live a godly life in Christ Jesus will be persecuted" (2 Timothy 3:12). Author Philip Yancey says that spreading the idea that becoming a Christian guarantees health and prosperity is the same argument that Satan advanced in the book of Job, which was decisively refuted.[9]

If we *do* expect health, wealth, and prosperity, it will be easy to doubt God's love for us when painful things happen. We may discover we believed it all along, by our outraged response when tragedy strikes: "How could a loving God let this happen?!" But if we acknowledge the existence of pain, however uncalled-for it may be, and accept the existence of the evil one who promotes evil, then we will be more likely to run to God for healing in times of trouble rather than scream at Him for failing us.

Kushner's book includes the perspective of an Auschwitz survivor, taken from Reeve Robert Brenner's book, *The Faith and Doubt of Holocaust Survivors*. It provides an awe-inspiring response to suffering:

It never occurred to me to question God's doings or lack of doings while I was an inmate of Auschwitz, although of course I understand others did . . . I was no less or no more religious because of what the Nazis did to us; and I believe my faith in God was not undermined in the least. It never occurred to me to associate the calamity we were experiencing with God, to blame Him, or to believe in Him less or cease believing in Him at all because He didn't come to our aid. God doesn't owe us that, or anything. We owe our lives to Him. If someone believes God is responsible for the death of six million because He didn't somehow do something to save them, he's got his thinking reversed. We owe God our lives for the few or many years we live, and we have the duty to worship Him and do as He commands us. That's what we're here on earth for, to be in God's service, to do God's bidding.[10]

With that said, let me say again that anger toward God is perfectly fine. Not only is it natural; it is also honest. No one, including God, expects us to fall at His feet in worship when atrocities happen. I think He certainly hopes we're able to worship Him in the midst of tragedy, but He is not disappointed in the times we simply can't, because He knows the pain we feel and our lack of understanding as to why terrible things happen.

Kushner handles our feelings of anger toward God with respect both to the person and to God. He states our anger won't hurt God, nor will it provoke Him to punish us for it. He believes that, unfortunately, our anger is falsely directed—that what has happened was not really God's fault. Anger can also become a barrier to seeking the comfort that religion can give. Getting angry at ourselves can lead to depression. Getting angry at others makes it hard for them to help us. Anger at the situation, because it is undeserved and unfair, is the most healthy way to release our emotions, because it discharges the anger without making it harder for us to get help.

Another emotion associated with pain, along with guilt and anger, is jealousy. It's natural to be jealous of others who have what we so deeply want, such as a husband to come home to, a baby to hold, or a son who returns alive and healthy from the war while ours was killed in action. It's not because we resent their good fortune but because it accentuates our own emptiness.

So how do we conquer this jealousy and emptiness? Kushner shares the old Chinese tale about the woman whose only son died. She went to the holy man hoping he had a prayer to bring her son back to life. Instead, he told her to fetch a mustard seed from a home that has never known sorrow so it could be used to drive the sorrow out of her life. In the course of her quest, the woman found that every home had sorrow. The sorrows she found touched her, and she stayed to minister to them. Eventually she was so involved in ministering to other people's grief that she forgot about her original quest for the magical mustard seed, never realizing that it had indeed driven the sorrow from her life.[11]

In addition to ministering to others, prayer is a great way to conquer pain and struggle. Kushner states that "people who pray for courage, for strength to bear the unbearable, for the grace to remember what they have left instead of what they have lost, very often find their prayers answered."[12]

To be honest with you, I did not pray that prayer often. Instead, I prayed for God to stop the pain. But when I did ask for courage, strength, and grace to be thankful for what I had left, God answered. Every time. Which is not to say it was easy, but I can proclaim that God was faithful. Believing in God did not lessen my pain, but my faith gave me hope. And hope led to peace.

Believing in God and heaven helped me to gradually understand that the pain was mine, not David's. Even considering how painful Kushner's son's illness and my son's illness were here on earth and also considering how much we prayed here on earth for a different outcome, believing in Christ's resurrection and an afterlife gives a different perspective. There are only healthy people in heaven. Eternity will be more joyful for having known pain on earth.

The unendurable is the beginning of the curve of joy.
—Djuna Barnes

God whispers to us in our pleasure,
speaks in our conscience,
but shouts in our pains.
It is His megaphone to rouse a deaf world.[13]
-C. S. Lewis

Meanwhile, Where Is God When It Hurts?

Consider it pure joy, my brothers, whenever you face
trials of many kinds, because you know that the testing
of your faith develops perseverance. Perseverance must
finish its work so that you may be mature and complete,
not lacking anything.
—James 1:2-4 NIV

Dear friends, do not be surprised at the painful trial
you are suffering, as though something strange
were happening to you. But rejoice that you participate
in the sufferings of Christ, so that you may be overjoyed
when his glory is revealed.
—1 Peter 4:12-13 NIV

For our light and momentary troubles are achieving for
us an eternal glory that far outweighs them all. So we fix
our eyes not on what is seen, but on what is unseen. For
what is seen is temporary, but what is unseen is eternal.
—2 Corinthians 4:17-18 NIV

These verses are not merely telling us to "look on the
bright side." Nor are they suggesting that suffering is good in
itself. Rather, they are encouraging us to focus on the value
of suffering and how it can change us. The spotlight is aimed
on the end result, the productive use God can make of the
suffering in our lives.[14]

But God needs our cooperation and the commitment of our trust to achieve that result. Rejoicing can be described as the process of giving Him that commitment. Philip Yancey points out that James does not say to rejoice in the trials but to "count it pure joy when you face trials." There is a major difference. The first celebrates the pain, the second celebrates the opportunity for growth produced by pain. We rejoice that the pain can be transformed. We rejoice in the object of our faith, God, who can bring about the transformation.[15]

Most Christians believe that when Jesus came as a baby, God entered human history fully. Like any human, He was subject to the laws and limitations of our planet. He was touched by the suffering He saw, and He always used His supernatural powers to heal, never to punish.[16]

In the beginning of the thirteenth chapter of Luke, Jesus was asked the question we often ponder, "Who caused this suffering?" Jesus emphatically says that the zealots killed by Pilate and the workers killed during construction were no more guilty or deserving of their suffering than anyone else. While not giving a specific cause of the death, Jesus makes it very clear it was not because of wrongdoing. He uses these tragedies to point to eternal truths relevant to all of us, the shortness of life and being ready to meet our Creator.[17]

In Luke 13, Jesus does, however, give the cause of a woman crippled by a spirit for eighteen years. He says she was bound by Satan. For the man born blind in John 9, Jesus vigorously states it was not the man's sin or his parent's sin, but so that God's work may be done in his life. Yancey points out that suffering gives the general warning to us all that there is something very wrong with our planet.[18]

When I was bewildered by David's illness, like countless others, I turned to the book of Job. Job suffered so much, and I'm sure he never understood the reason for his many tragedies. Still he ended up believing that (1) he did not deserve all his suffering and (2) God still deserved his loyalty.

Following thirty-five chapters of debate on the problem of pain, God does not answer one question or explain Job's suffering to him. Instead, in the beautiful speech in chapters 38-41, God shows the marvels of the physical world he created.

Clearly God created a world beyond our understanding. Job's reply: "Surely I spoke of things I did not understand, things too wonderful for me to know" (Job 42:3 NIV). This statement of trust pleased God. Job concluded that a God wise enough and good enough to create this beautiful world was able to take care of him.

Satan had challenged God that Job loved God for the prosperity God gave him and the hedge of protection around him. But Job chose to love the Giver, not just the gifts. It's a question worth posing: do we love the Giver or the gifts?

Yancey quotes Rabbi Abraham Heschel, who wrote, "Faith like Job's cannot be shaken because it is the result of having already been shaken."[19]

There is no reason to believe that our purpose lies in life, liberty, and the pursuit of happiness. There are no scriptural passages to support this idea. Rather, we are here to be changed, to become more like God so we are prepared for our eternal life with Him. Suffering can become something of value through this process.

In fact, suffering can teach us the value of dependence. Yancey states that unless we learn dependence, we will never experience grace. In 2 Corinthians 12, the apostle Paul gave an example of this principle from his own personal experience. He had a "thorn in the flesh," an unidentified ailment for which many possibilities have been suggested—eye disease, chronic depression, malaria, sexual temptation, or epilepsy. The process he outlines applies for all our various thorns in the flesh.[20]

At first, Paul resented the torment of affliction since it interfered with his busy ministry schedule and caused him to question God. He pleaded for a miracle of healing three times. Each time his request was denied. Lastly, he received the message that God wanted him to learn through his suffering: "My grace is sufficient for you, for my power is made perfect in weakness" (2 Corinthians 12:9 NIV).

Paul's benefit from this nagging weakness was that it kept him dependent on God and not on himself. When he realized this, his attitude changed from fighting his "thorn in the flesh" to accepting it. He changed his pleas to God from removing his thorn to praying for God to redeem or transform the pain to his benefit. Typical of his personality, once Paul had learned this lesson, he began boasting about his weakness. To an audience impressed by power and physical appearance, he bragged about God choosing the lowly and weak of the world to confound the wise and strong. This was the lesson of the beatitudes: sorrow, poverty, and weakness can be means of grace if we turn to God with a humble, dependent spirit. Paul concluded, "For when I am weak, then I am strong."[21]

When we trust God in the midst of our suffering, a deeper level of faith can be developed. This can transform our suffering into lasting, eternal qualities. Yancey inspired me with these words: "Where is God when it hurts? He is in *us*—not in the things that hurt—helping to transform bad into good. We can safely say that God brings good out of evil; we cannot say that God brings about the evil in hopes of producing good."[22]

When Christ died, God was in Christ, reconciling the world to Himself. Yancey states, "In Luther's phrase the cross showed 'God struggling with God.' If Jesus was a mere man, his death would prove God's cruelty; the fact that he was God's Son proves instead that God fully identifies with suffering humanity. On the cross, God himself absorbed the awful pain of this world."[23]

> The first step to healing is not a step away
> from the pain, but a step toward it.[24]
> —Henri Nouwen

From Darkness to Light

Death is as natural as birth, and loss is inevitable. Jerry Sittser, author of *A Grace Disguised*, lost three generations instantly when a tragic car accident killed his mother, his wife, and his daughter. My first thought when I read his book was if losing one loved one is horrible, losing three loved ones must be three times as horrible.

Sittser deals with the question, whose loss is worse? He differentiates between normal, natural curable loss and irreversible, catastrophic loss such as "terminal illness, disability, divorce, rape, emotional abuse, physical and sexual abuse, chronic unemployment, crushing disappointment, mental illness, and ultimately death." These losses are permanent with cumulative consequences and immeasurable impact. The normal losses may be compared to a broken bone, the catastrophic losses to an amputation.[25]

It's natural to compare our loss with another's. The problem is we never really understand the depth of the other's suffering. When I witnessed the toll bipolar took on David's life as my family suffered with him, there were times when I thought that, given the choice, I would prefer practically any chronic physical illness over a serious chronic mental illness. Yet when I considered the years of caregiving, thousands of dollars, and constant attention and problems that serious injuries and illness can require, I realized it is impossible to compare.

We are alike in our grief. Sittser's grief journey intimately mirrored my own grief journey. When mental illness struck my family, one truth hit me right smack in the middle of my gut—I may not get what I want out of this pain, but no matter where it leads me, I *can* learn from it.

What choice do we have? While we would never choose pain or loss, we can choose how we will "play with the cards we are dealt," as Paul said to me when I visited David at the hospital after his breakdown.

We cannot spare ourselves the grief from our loss, but the sickness of the soul can heal. Sittser speaks of the power of response. "Response involves the *choices* we make, the *grace* we receive, and ultimately the *transformation* we experience in the loss . . . If we face loss squarely and respond to it wisely, we will actually become healthier people, even as we draw closer to physical death."[26] He feels our souls will be healed as they can only be healed through suffering.

People who gradually move beyond the "Why?" to "What meaning can I derive from this suffering?" will allow themselves to be transformed by their suffering and will become more sensitive to the pain of other people.

Sittser shares from Viktor Frankl's book *Man's Search for Meaning.* Frankl discovered from personal experience during his years in Nazi death camps during World War II that some prisoners used power of choice to determine how they would respond to their circumstances and displayed courage, dignity, and inner strength. They were able to transcend their suffering. In spite of all the evidence to the contrary, some chose to believe in God, to believe in a better day tomorrow even though there was little promise of this. They chose to love, in spite of the hateful environment in which they had to live.

Frankl concluded that because these prisoners found meaning in their suffering, they were able to transcend their experience. "If there is meaning in life at all, then there must be a meaning in suffering. Suffering is an ineradicable part of life, even as fate and death. Without suffering and death human life cannot be complete."[27]

When we experience loss, darkness can invade our soul. Light can invade it also. Both work together in our transformation. We are powerless to hold off the darkness. Sittser writes, "Sudden and tragic loss leads to terrible darkness. It is as inescapable as nightmares during a high fever. The darkness comes, no matter how hard we try to hold it off. However threatening, we must face it, and we must face it alone."[28]

Eventually, light comes. Without darkness, how can we see the light?

Jerry Sittser recounts in his book a dream in which he was frantically running west to catch the warmth and light of the setting sun. His cousin told him that though east and west seem farthest removed on a map, they meet eventually on a globe. His sister later told him the quickest way to reach the sun is to plunge east into darkness until you come to the light of the sunrise. Sittser then decided to go into the darkness and let the experience of his loss take him wherever the journey led and allow the suffering to transform him rather than try to avoid it. He chose to go in the direction of the pain and yield to the loss even though he had no idea at the time what that would mean.[29]

This decision was his first step toward pain, but also the first step toward growth. For months he looked at the car accident that suddenly killed three loved ones—his wife, his daughter, and his mother. He stared at the accident and relived its trauma. This caused acute depression, bewilderment, and exhaustion. The result was sorrow that took up permanent residence in his soul and enlarged it. Darkness invaded his soul, but so did the light. This helped him enter into a new and different life.[30]

When I was maybe eight years old, my elder sister told me there are "growing pains." She said that when our bodies grow, it hurts. While I doubt there is scientific evidence for this theory, I certainly believe there are growing pains in our souls. I came to believe this most fiercely through the loss of David.

I attended LOSS meetings (Loved Ones Surviving Suicide) for many months. My friends asked me, "You say it is so painful to go to LOSS. Why do you keep going?" My answer: "I feel I have to face the pain and loss. Then in the long run I can heal. It helps me to embrace my pain and empathize with others."

There was no escape from the pain and sorrow. I also felt I was facing the weakness of my human nature. Yet I felt I must resist the natural impulse and run toward the pain, not away from it. The experience of pain must not define our lives. Our response must define our lives.

*   *   *

There is no way out of the desert except through it.
—African proverb

Grief feels and looks like a desert—barren, dry, harsh, vast. You can't go over it, you can't go under it; the only way is to go through it. Grief needs to be felt, expressed, and experienced. Repressed grief can lead to serious clinical depression.

Dr. Robert R. Thompson states that delayed or unresolved grief responses can torment until, in one form or another, the person eventually relives the traumatic death of a loved one by seeking help through therapy or other means of finding resolution.

Dr. Thompson also states the death of a child or sibling can, by itself, lead to serious clinical depression. In cases where sadness overwhelms or physical symptoms persist, help from a mental health professional should be sought. This "involutional" depression requires medication and perhaps even hospitalization. It is important for those who associate with someone who has experienced the tragic loss of a child, spouse, or sibling to gently urge a person showing symptoms of this treatable form of depression to seek treatment or other forms of intervention, as you would for any other form of illness.[31]

Feelings of bitterness, despair, and hatred are natural after catastrophic loss. We have to struggle against them for a long time to keep them from dominating us. The struggle can lead to release. We must decide to *not* allow destructive emotions to conquer us. Our emotions seem real to us, but they are not reality. We need to acknowledge our feelings, own them, and declare that they not reality. God is the center of reality. Surrendering to God will give us a sense of hope in the midst of pain.

Even though tragedy is random and seems senseless at the time, it may fit into a plan that our imaginations could not envision. In the biblical story, Joseph was sold into slavery by his brothers and endured many years of imprisonment. Joseph endured and acknowledged the evil done to him. Yet Joseph saw a bigger purpose when he said to his brothers, "You intended to harm me, but God intended it for good to accomplish what is now being done, the saving of many lives" (Genesis 50:20 NIV).

Over lunch with a friend, who is also a suicide survivor, I lamented, "David's illness and death obliterated the sense of control I once had. There has to be a purpose for bipolar and the pain my family suffered from David's death. It has to make sense." She said, "If you find a reason that works for you, it can be true for you." I repeated, "There has to be a purpose." Her reply: "The important thing is there is purpose for you."

While he was talking to me, my doctor's nurse came in
and said, "Doctor, there is a man here who thinks he is invisible."
The doctor said, "Tell him I can't see him."[32]

Strangers, Church, and Prayer

Pastor Dan's wife, Cheryl, was very busy fielding calls and answering questions immediately after David's death. When I called her to arrange the time to meet with Pastor Dan at the mortuary to plan the funeral, I asked for prayer. She answered with her usual uplifting and straightforward manner, "I don't have a very direct line to God."

How many of us feel like we do?

It is natural to turn to God in prayer at a time of need. We talk to God and we believe He listens, but when prayer requests are repeated urgently over many years (or a lifetime), we wonder if God hears *every* prayer. I remembered my prayers for David, his illness, his life, his faith, and the outcome that shocked me and rocked my whole family.

I attended many meetings where evangelists stated that with enough faith, we would all be healed. It sounded so encouraging and uplifting. Young and idealistic (and naive), I wanted to believe, and so I believed. Now I know that many prayers for healing are not answered.

Attending church was painful for several months after David's death. There were too many memories of David: his baptism, confirmation, Sunday school classes, John and I sitting in the pews with pride as he recited his piece or sang or played the piano. But I kept going back. Old habits die hard, and I clung to them like a bulldog to a bone. I needed church. It was comforting to sit beside John, sharing the hymnbook, sharing our faith, and sharing our loss. Though I often felt dazed, John kept me on track in the bulletin, the hymnbook, and other mundane details of the ritual I knew so well. The ritual and liturgy were comforting, reassuring us that even though our lives were changed, some things don't change.

Going out in public was also difficult for several months. People were talking, carefree. I felt different and lonely. The first year most of my social life was with family and close friends and a few people in whom I sensed a sensitive and caring personality. However, I did enjoy getting acquainted with strangers in the ladies' dressing room at the Northfield Senior Center after swimming. As I chatted with the friendly women, the subject turned to how scripture gives us varying messages at different times in our lives, at a different age, and with changing experiences.

I pondered Romans 8:26-28 (NIV): "The Spirit helps us in our weakness. We do not know what we ought to pray for, but the Spirit himself intercedes for us with groans that words cannot express. And he who searches our hearts knows the mind of the Spirit, because the Spirit intercedes for the saints in accordance with God's will. And we know that in all things God works for the good of those who love him, who have been called according to his purpose."

How does the Holy Spirit make intercession for us? After my talk with the strangers in the dressing room, the meaning seemed more clear. Sometimes we have no idea what to say. At such a time, a wiser, kind friend, the Spirit of God helps us. When we have no words in our grief, God understands. He even prays for us when we don't feel we can. I sometimes sat with my hands outstretched asking God to pray for me.

Loss changes us. We are different persons. We know God through what we suffer. If everyone's prayers were answered according to their desires, there would be no need for faith. I had said many prayers for David to be able to live with his illness as a productive person. I got the opposite of what I prayed for. There was no miracle to avert a tragedy, but people helped me, and I was able to draw on a strength outside myself to survive life's unfairness. God did not send the tragedy. He provided the strength to get through it. I believe God heard my prayers.

Our good friend, Anonymous, explains it this way:

I cannot do without Thee
I cannot stand alone
I have no strength or goodness
Nor wisdom of my own
But Thou, Beloved Savior
Art all in all to me
And perfect strength in weakness
Is mine when I lean on Thee.
—Anonymous

* * *

The unfathomable mystery of God is that God is a Lover
who wants to be loved. The one who created us is waiting for
our response to the love that gave us our being.[33]
—Henri Nouwen

Adapt

After David's death, something friends showered me with besides food, hugs, kind concern, and encouraging words was books. One of the authors was Barbara Johnson, who writes from the heart about experiences that would break any heart. She lost two of her four sons on the brink of adulthood. Then she also suffered estrangement from another son when she lashed out at him with anger, even hatred, when she learned of his homosexuality.

Her Christian counselor told her there would be little success in changing the sexual orientation of her homosexual son, that there was no miraculous "fix." But what I consider a bigger miracle is God's grace in giving her the ability to "accept, adapt, understand, and, above all, to love unconditionally."[34] If unconditional love isn't a miracle, what is?

An earlier chapter of this book gives information on the stages of grief and loss. Barbara Johnson gives my favorite version in her inimitable humorous, light, but meaningful style:

- First, we churn. This is sort of like having your insides ground up by a meat grinder.
- Second, we burn. Shock gives way to burning anger, which is a consuming fire. [After David's death, I wondered how the first visitor at the visitation line knew I would need to scream—at the top of my lungs.]
- Third, we yearn. We remember the "good old days" when life was good, problems were minor and quickly passed. We know we can't return to that time, yet this stage may last longer than any other.

- Fourth, we learn. We learn what we are made of. We learn from others. The values we have always taken for granted become more than just nice theories. The pain makes us more understanding and compassionate and integrates our spiritual values into who we are.
- Last, we turn our problems over to God. We realize all our thinking, talking, and feeling are not enough. Life may be unreasonable and hard, but we can hand it over to the One who is still in control. Whatever God allows He will get us through somehow.[35]

It would be nice if we could get through these five stages and be done with it, like learning to ride a bike or swim, but it doesn't work that way. The truth is we never really "arrive." Still, we can keep moving through the five stages again and again to where the painful stages are shorter and less often.

When I was struggling to accept David's illness and its impact on his life and our families, I remember thinking at one time, *Whew, I've reached stage 5*. Then several months later, the unbelievable happened—David died by suicide.

Johnson cautions that you can reach stage 5 and believe you've turned it over to God and the very next day be back churning or burning or yearning. It still happens to her from time to time, but she finds that she's in those painful stages less often and for shorter times.[36]

Her honesty is encouraging. I regress, but like her I can go back and try again and again. To me, life is a lot like baseball. God gives us a lot of strikes to get around the bases before we make it "home." Don't count the strikes. Keep your bat up, your eye on the ball, and swing!

Johnson gives practical advice on learning and turning. The key word on this is *adapt*. She distinguishes between accepting the pain that life brings and *adapting* to the challenges that pain may bring. By adapting to your problems rather than blindly accepting them, you are able to work on changing what you can. Complete acceptance can keep you from putting effort into what you can change.[37]

She gives the example of Candlelighters, a group made up of parents whose children have cancer. They have chosen to bring in light by supporting each other in adapting to the terrible pain surrounding these families instead of cursing their darkness of ongoing pain and suffering.[38]

NAMI (the National Alliance on Mental Illness), a nonprofit organization dedicated to improving the lives of individuals with mental illness by offering education, support, and advocacy to them and their families, is another example of lighting a candle instead of cursing the darkness, stigma, and pain of the disease.

Adapting includes changing our attitude. We mothers often think that with our age, wisdom, and love, we should be able to "fix" or "change" our children to help them live happy and productive lives according to the values we have tried to instill. Again, practical Barbara quashes this idealistic notion with a reminder: "Where there is no control, there is no responsibility."

After eighteen years of building our values into our children, they are no longer our responsibility. Our sons and daughters have free choice. Barbara follows this with a note of hope. Our children can do their own thing, but "God can pull their tail whenever He wants to."[39]

Adaptability is essential for a healthy life, even in the midst of chronic disease and unsolvable problems. If we don't *adapt* to the changing circumstances of our lives, our well-being will deteriorate even more.[40]

Barbara Johnson tells of Michael Malloy, director of Christian Counseling Services in Nashville, Tennessee, who attended a seminar conducted by Dr. Larry Crabb, a Christian psychologist and author. Dr. Crabb asked the group, "Do you use God to solve your problems? Or do you use your problems to find God?"[41]

We may apply biblical principles in hopes of solving everything, and we can hear testimonies of God helping others and hope He'll help us too, but we can't assume that's how it works every time. We may do this, but our problems may not be alleviated or may even get worse.

However, when we "use our problems to find God," we aren't looking for the quick fix; we are learning something about the "theology of suffering." Michael Malloy wrote, "Those who suffer well and keep a passion for God in the midst of their pain are often called saints."[42]

In support groups I have heard the people talk of "tribulation." This is not one hard blow, but one blow followed by another and another. When you are in pain, you wait hopefully for God to act. You hope and wait and hope and wait some more. King David knew what it felt like to be in trouble up to his neck and beyond when he wrote Psalm 69:1-3. His floods were overwhelming, he was weary with calling for help, his eyes were failing with looking (hopefully) for God.

As the waters seem to be coming over your head, nothing hurts as much as when Christians who are not dealing with the problems we face offer glib answers like "Just praise the Lord, learn to trust Him in all things." At such a time you don't need a challenge; you need comfort.

During trials we wonder if we have enough faith. I certainly did. Then I remembered that Jesus said we only need a little faith, a mustard seed of faith. He said just a mustard seed will grow into a mighty tree. One night I wrote a little prayer and stuck it by my bedside:

> Dear God,
> How could you ask this of me?
> My faith cannot move this mountain
> My faith could not climb this mountain
> But with this mustard seed of faith
> I will cling to my mountain today.
>
> Your child,
> Pat Day

> P.S. I was tempted to sign this like the apostle John, "Your favorite child," but I know better.

> The secret things belong unto the Lord our God:
> but those things which are revealed
> belong unto us and our children forever,
> that we may do all the words of this law.
> **—Deuteronomy 29:29 KJV**

Most Richly Blessed

I asked God for strength, that I might achieve.
I was made weak, that I might learn humbly to obey.
I asked for health, that I might do greater things.
I was given infirmity, that I might do better things.
I asked for riches, that I might be happy.
I was given poverty, that I might be wise.
I asked for power, that I might have the praise of others.
I was given weakness, that I might feel the need of God.
I asked for all things, that I might enjoy life.
I was given life, that I might enjoy all things.
I got nothing I asked for—
but everything I had hoped for.
Almost despite myself, my
unspoken prayers were answered.
I am, among all people,
most richly blessed.

—Anonymous Confederate soldier

CHAPTER 11

Epilogue
The Day Will Come

Every beginning has an end. Every end has a beginning. When David's life here on earth ended, it was the beginning of grief, regret, and eventually acceptance, growth, and renewed purpose. His life showed that mental illness is a serious, life-threatening disease. His achievements and courage in the midst of his illness will inspire many.

I can and will move on with my life, but I will never leave David behind. Some issues of his life and death will never be resolved by me or by my family. There will always be photos, songs, and memories that trigger pain. That is our connection to David and we don't want to lose it.

In this sense, there will never be a time of acceptance. Though I will ever be thankful for David and the great gift that his life, however difficult, was to my family.

It is impossible to understand why suffering happens. I asked, "Why?" countless times after David died. But in the course of my wondering, I discovered that it is possible to regain peace after a tragedy, by embracing the knowledge that peace comes "not as the world gives but from the Lord" and accepting the fact that some questions cannot be answered. Doing that enabled me to move on.

David's death also made me even more aware and accepting of my own mortality. With this came a desire to live each day as fully as possible with more appreciation of the beauty in people and the world and more sadness for the cruelty and suffering.

Have you ever wondered, when we pass on from this earth, will we remember some of the things from our earthly life? Is it possible if we remember our pain that the light and presence of God will be more joyful? I do not know, but it is one of the things I want to talk about when I get there.

In the midst of my grieving, it was difficult to imagine that life could ever become normal again, that I would ever again enjoy simple pleasures, or truly laugh again. But as time has passed, I have learned firsthand it *is* possible to enjoy life again. To eat a good meal and taste its deliciousness, to walk in the sunshine and be grateful for the warmth on your skin, to laugh with joy, to gaze at the sunrise and sunset in awe, to inhale the fresh morning air.

And the day will also come for all of you who are suffering a loss. The color will return to your world. You, like me, will be glad you are alive.

> The Lord will be your everlasting life,
> and your days of sorrow will end.
> —Isaiah 60:20 NIV

What Was the Father Thinking?

Intellectually we know the Heavenly Father paid a great price when He gave His only begotten Son as payment for our sins that we may be cleansed in His blood and righteousness and be His forgiven children.

Many weep when their loved ones go to war. They know they face possible death. They know they may return wounded. They know that they will not be the same people when they return, that there will be emotional scars, if not physical ones.

What was God the Father thinking when He sent His Son to earth? He knew Jesus would die, but he also knew the good that would come from it—eternal life without pain or tears for us. No, it cannot be scientifically proven there is an afterlife, any more than it can be proven there is not one. Though there is the evidence and the influence of the sinless life and resurrection of Jesus.

Many behold the power and wonder of nature and believe in a Creator and Sustainer. When I consider just one aspect of nature, the way a seed goes into the earth, flourishes, reproduces, and dies, I think it takes as much faith to not believe in immortality as it does to believe in it.

Our human life begins as a seed. Jesus began His life as a seed too before He grew in stature and wisdom. Before we can grow into adulthood, we have many "facts of life" to learn. I recall a friend's response when his wife told him of a misfortune: "Life happens." Perhaps you've seen the bumper stickers that state this fact of life in a more earthy fashion. "Shit happens." That phrase has many meanings to me as a farmer's wife.

Manure doesn't smell, look, or feel good. Yet it can be used to promote growth of our soul. Flowers can grow on dung hills. If you are alive, you will experience loss and unwanted change. It will hurt and you will grieve.

God can seem distant (or nonexistent) at such times. Yet some instinctively turn to God, knowing they need someone greater than themselves. Many become angry. I know I did. But it finally dawned on me my faith was being tested in the darkness. Until we are tested, how do we know if our faith is genuine? If you feel you have failed the faith test, there is no need to worry. Your faith can be rekindled. When I read the Gospels, I see Jesus as the most forgiving person who ever lived on this earth. You may too.

When life hits us with a painful loss, we must encourage each other to grieve and move on, cherishing the gifts we have been given and the gifts we still have. With hope we can live and love again. I did. And so can you. But we need each other. And we need God.

The song sung at David's funeral gives a hint of what I think the afterlife contains. May the words also soothe the pain of any loss you have endured.

HYMN OF PROMISE

In the bulb there is a flower; in the seed, an apple tree;
In cocoons, a hidden promise: butterflies will soon be free!
In the cold and snow of winter there's a spring that waits to be,
Unrevealed until its season, something God alone can see.
There's a song in every silence, seeking word and melody;
There's a dawn in every darkness, bringing hope to you and me.
From the past will come the future; what it holds, a mystery,
Unrevealed until its season, something God alone can see.
In our end is our beginning; in our time, infinity;
In our doubt there is believing; in our life, eternity.
In our death, a resurrection; at the last, a victory.
Unrevealed until its season, something God alone can see.[1]

David's illness and death planted a seed in my heart for better understanding, acceptance, and compassion for mental illness. This book grew from that seed. My hope and prayer is that the seed will grow to fruition in its own time.

The Lord will fulfill his purpose for me.
Psalms 138:8

Nothing that is worth doing can be achieved in a lifetime;
therefore we must be saved by hope.
Reinhold Niebuhr

Questions to David

David, I want to talk to you one more time because I have questions to ask.

David, was your suicide a decision or a result of the illness? Had you any idea how much your family would grieve your death?

Or could you see only your own pain? I would find that easy to understand. You suffered much from the illness and all you lost because of it. Looking over my notes, I better understand the extent of your loss. Yes, I kept notes on everything. Did you ever notice that?

When I was still working at St. Olaf, your psychiatrist called me, and in her calm, pleasant voice gave me terrible news. She said that your illness was serious, that if you had a severe episode, it could end in death by suicide.

Her words scared the life out of me. I went home and talked to John about it. We felt that we would keep on keeping on, hoping for the best. We knew you had been a survivor through many troubles. We believed we knew you much better than the psychiatrist.

In my pain I do not understand. Please know one thing. I do not blame you. I cannot blame you. Remember that song we often sang at the end of our church service?

> Turn your eyes upon Jesus,
> Look full in His wonderful face,
> And the things of earth will grow strangely dim
> In the light of His glory and grace.

I've written another version:

> Lord, open our eyes that we may see Jesus.
> That we may look through His eyes of love.
> See the suffering of the person beside us.
> And reach out our hands to comfort and heal.

> Lord, open our eyes to see you in others,
> Those who weep and those who laugh.

Touch our eyes that we may see
Our neighbors with eyes of love.

Till we meet at that Wonderful Place,
Good night, David,
See you in the morning,

Mom

APPENDIX

Letters of Comfort

FROM SHARON AND DICK (SISTER AND BROTHER-IN-LAW)

Wish we could do more to ease your burden. Surely miss David's smile, intelligence, good humor, and caring nature. His absence has left a void that can never be filled, but we must hold on to each other as best we can.

FROM MELISSA GARNER (DAVID'S FRIEND)

Dear Pat and John, and Matt and Mike and Danny,

I am very sorry for your loss. David's always been such a great friend to me, always willing to listen (and interrupt with questions!) and always willing to help me however he could and whenever I asked. I'll miss him every week when I don't see him, the next time I need something good to read, the next time I buy art. And the next time I read the *Onion*, of course.

David charmed every one of my friends that he met, and they'll all miss him too.

Please do let me know if there's any way I can help you during this impossible time. I promise to keep in touch. Love,

FROM BECKY ELLERASS (DAVID'S COUSIN)

Dear Pat, John, Mike, Matt, and Danny,

Our deepest thoughts and prayers are with you all at this time. We pray that God will be with you for all the ups and downs of emotions you are, and will be feeling. He will never leave you.

Please know that we are here for you and would love to help in any way.

Pat and John, David was a wonderful person. I think of how he had such a KIND AND GENTLE HEART. He was so easygoing and always seemed to have a smile on his face. When you talked to him, his eyes always seemed to light up. He was so loving, kind, gentle, witty with a great sense of humor and always ready to listen. I remember him as a great listener. I know it takes two wonderful people to create such a wonderful man, and I know that David felt blessed to have you both as his parents.

Mike, Matt, and Danny . . . there probably aren't too many things that are stronger than the bond between brothers. I bet you all have a million memories stored up—some good, some bad—but all of them so special and meaningful in their own way. I know David felt blessed to have you all as his brothers, to call you family. Many people go through life never experiencing what you have, that brotherly bond. I'm grateful David had you all.

We carry fond memories of David with us. We love you and hold you in our prayers. Love,

FROM SUE AND JEANE ROHLAND, BILL SKALLY, KEN GOLD (OWNERS OF APARTMENTS THAT DAVID MANAGED)

Dear Pat, John (Mike, Matt, Dan, and Kasumi),

Thank you so much for the beautiful letter and photograph of David! So often we have wondered how you all are doing and have wanted to call you or write but did not know if we should.

Your letter has been a help to us—we want you to know that we miss David. Perhaps a bit selfishly too—he was wonderful at the building. But more than that, we miss him, his personality, his sense of caring.

It is good to know that you are coping all right. While we did not have the privilege of knowing David as a family member, when we read your letter, it brought David back so clearly. He was amazing in how he handled his illness! Our friend Pam (and Jeanne too) have worked in the mental health field and they say that bipolar disorder is a truly horrible illness. And David always had his sense of humor and his care and concern for other people. (We smiled when we read the obituary where it talked about David on the busload of nuns going to the protest!)

One of the things we said was that if the loss of David was horrible for us—we could not imagine what his family was going through. That is why we were so happy to receive your letter and to know that you are all right. Your words were so true when you wrote David was a wonderful gift and the greater the gift, the harder the loss.

Pat and John—thank you for your wonderful son!

FROM HETAL DALAL (DAVID'S FRIEND)

Dear Mr. and Mrs. Day,

I am writing because your son David was a friend of mine, and I am sad, so sad, to learn that he is gone. David and I went to law school together—we were in the same section that first year, and by the alphabet as well as personality, we were destined to be friends.

His dogged pursuit of a matter made him stand out, and it was always a pleasure to debate and spar with him. He had such a keen mind, and a way of handling obscurity with a plumb. I miss him so.

Dave helped me paint my house—his careless splotches still decorate the woodwork in the hallway. Once, after a bike ride at Cannon Falls trail, he brought me to your farm, and Mr. Day took us on a tour.

Then we finished law school, and I had kids and he moved to Florida. We lost sight of each other, but never (at least to me) lost sight that he was a friend. It would mean a lot to me to visit you and talk about Dave. If this would not be too troubling, would you call me or write. I only have this address.

My best to you both. You are in my thoughts.

FROM MARILYN OTTE (FRIEND)

Dear Pat,

My dear friend, my heart aches for you and your family. To say "my thoughts are with you" is at times the only thing I can think of to say. My heart goes out to you during these difficult days. Pat, you are an amazing woman. You share with us women how difficult your birthday was, then you can so wonderfully compliment me! What a wonderful friend you are!

I so admire the courage you and John have shown through these past months, but especially at the time of David's death, when you told others he suffered from bipolar, the truth of his death, the beautifully written story of his life. Love,

FROM SARA LATHROP (DAVID'S FRIEND)

Dear Mr. and Mrs. Day,

I am writing to tell you how very sorry I was to hear of your son David's death. I wish I had heard earlier. I saw the listing in the U of M Law School Alumni magazine.

David and I were in the same smaller "section" too. We had a study group together our first year as well. David always had a great, sunny outlook on life and on the law, and I liked him very much. He really stood out as an intelligent, caring, focused individual. He was always very sweet and supportive of me and I was fond of him. I am so saddened by his passing and so sorry for your loss.

FROM NANCY CANTWELL

Dear Pat and John,

I want you to know how much I have thought of you since reading about your son in the *Northfield News*. Because he was so extraordinary, I am afraid it made it even harder for you all to lose him. It does seem, however, that he wasted hardly a moment of his life, and that he sensed your support all along the way.

It was heartening just to read about him. Thank you for letting us all know what you wrote. I'll continue to hold him, and you, in my thoughts. Sincerely,

FROM MARGARET (FRIEND)

Dear Pat and John,

Thinking of you—and remembering what a special person David was. You can always be very proud of him!

You may not be far enough along in your grief process for this quote yet—but I hope someday you can feel this way: "Don't cry because it's over; smile because it happened."

—Dr. Seuss

David was a very special "*happening!*"

FROM ANN (FRIEND)

Dear Pat and John,

I can't begin to tell you how saddened we were to hear of David's death. We *do* know what it is like to lose a son and know it is extremely difficult to even keep functioning. When our son Jeff died, I hurt so bad for so long that I never thought I'd react normally to pain again.

I finally accepted Jeff's death when I realized the pain was *mine*, not Jeff's. I truly believe that he is safe in the loving arms of our heavenly father, just as I am sure David is. I still hurt for those of us who have only memories of our sons, but I praise God that we have those memories.

Our deepest sympathy, much love,

FROM NANCY SOTH

To John and Pat Day

I write to say how sorry I am to learn that David had passed away on April 19. I didn't know David, but I am so grateful to you for having told the *Northfield News* readers so much about him. It was a wonderful obituary, and I don't believe anyone could have read it without feeling loving and admiring of such a person and of his family.

Thank you so very much for creating this sweet memorial to David. I regret that I haven't had the experience of having him in my life as well. But I seriously doubt if I shall ever forget him. With gratitude,

FROM ARCH AND MARY LEEAN (FRIENDS) ON THE ONE-YEAR ANNIVERSARY OF DAVID'S DEATH

Dear Pat and John,

We've been thinking of you a lot—knowing that this April is an especially painful time. I don't know of any way that it can be much less painful. Not having David in your life is a daily loss.

I have been trying to learn to live in an attitude of gratitude for all that Sharon was to us and to others. But there is a huge feeling of missing so much—excitement, humor, joy, challenge that Sharon brought to us. Life is not as rich and satisfying as it was.

But, after five years, I can say the gut-wrenching pain has diminished.

Perhaps, someday, all of this will make sense to all of us.

We pray God will send you comfort, hope, and a sense of his presence—especially now. Love,

FROM BERNIE AND BERT REESE (SISTER AND BROTHER-IN-LAW) ON THE ONE-YEAR ANNIVERSARY OF DAVID'S DEATH

David entered into this world in 1971.
He took his place along with two brothers, in the Day family's
Who's Who. But David held his own.
As a mediator and friend, he often set the tone.
David was a happy boy and curious from the start.
He was a cowboy early on, a cowboy with a heart!
As David grew and spread his wings,
He touched a lot of hearts.
College years took him to a variety of schools,
But found his niche at Morris U.
There he excelled in many things and finished
Near the top of his class.
David achieved a lot of things that many only dream of.

His smarts aside, it was his thoughtful,
loving nature that drew people to him.
His great computer skills aside, it was his
Compassion and personality that were great.
His wonderful smile, his quick retort,
Are long to be remembered.
My occasional phone calls to David always
Left me with a smile. We would laugh a lot,
Do some sharing, and lift each other up.
He loved cars to drive, but not to fix,
And could share these times of dilemma with his dad.
He tested his mom with his exotic ideas
And questions—and they usually ended
Up with a bike ride.
We like to remember David as a wonderful gift
To his family and to our family.
Let us uphold his memory, and
Uphold our families, with the love and
Courage that David displayed
Throughout his lifetime.
We do have a wonderful family you know!

AND FROM PAT AND JOHN DAY TO FRIENDS IN RESPONSE

My dear friends,

I have started a letter to you a couple of times in my head. Thank you for the gift you gave as a memorial for David. And *all* your food was delicious and comforting—the meatballs, soup, that delicious cake with sinfully good frosting. We are fortunate to have good friends like you two. We don't understand the whys, but we can trust that God will someday (possibly not in this lifetime) reveal His answers.

We have searched for answers. A friend (who is a lifelong nurse) shared at a wedding we recently attended that she considered suicide a disease in itself, that it is an illness, not a choice. David has struggled painfully for the past eight years with bipolar disorder.

Our family is proud of David and the way he handled his devastating illness with his usual upbeat attitude, never losing his delightful sense of humor and kindly concern for others in the midst of the trials his illness inflicted. As one of David's friends put it, "He was a gentle soul with a terrific laugh." He was always a life-loving person.

A friend told me she checked the Internet and learned that for a severe case like David had, the suicide rate is 50 percent. We feel David had an illness he could not control.

Recently I talked to an acquaintance who suffers from bipolar. I knew she had had several breakdowns but did not know she had bipolar. After David was diagnosed, I read several books on mental illness, but I can honestly say I felt that I learned more about the disease from my brief talk with her. I wish I had known of her illness and talked to her about it eight years ago.

No one can completely know the suffering and anxiety and desires of another person. Sometimes I think only God completely understands our needs and trials. Even though this illness was not His will, I believe He can help us in our sorrow.

David was a wonderful gift, and the greater gift, the harder the loss. We will all miss David. His brothers feel they have lost a lifelong friend. There is so much we don't understand, but we hope that in God's plan, David completed his necessary earthly duties in his thirty-three years. We give thanks to God for the gift of his life!

All our crops John planted look good, although with this hot weather we could use rain. I have frozen thirty bags of peas and made rhubarb desserts and jam. John planted soybeans after the peas were harvested. If we get some rain soon and have a nice fall, the bean crop will give a second crop on the same land. Our flowers and hosta have never looked better because of the cool, wet weather in early summer.

May God bless and reward you for your kindness!
With love,

ENDNOTES

Dedication

1. Lines 5 and 6 come from a statement by Harold S. Kushner that struck a chord in my heart (When Bad Things Happen to Good People [New York: Schocken Books, 1981], 5.

Chapter 1

1. Author's note: This poem and essay was inspired by one whose origin I cannot recall, which expressed the idea that we see Jesus in people who perform acts of kindness and love.

Chapter 6

1. Addressing Mental Health: You or Someone You Love May Need Help," Health Journal, BlueCross, BlueShield Plus of Minnesota, 15, no. 1 (Spring 2006).
2. What is Mental Illness: Mental Illness Facts," p. 1, http://www.nami.org/PrinterTemplate.cfm?Section =About_Mental_Illness&Templ.html (accessed April 26, 2008).
3. Ibid., 1.
4. Sue Abderholden, executive director, NAMI of Minnesota, "Sometimes the Mental Health System, Not the Parent, Is the Problem," *St. Paul Pioneer Press* (October 18, 2006), 10B.
5. "What Is Mental Illness: Mental Illness Facts," p. 1.
6. Ibid.
7. Ibid.
8. Denise Gellene, "Mental Health Keeping Us Home," *St. Paul Pioneer Press* (October 7, 2007), 15A.
9. "What Is Mental Illness: Mental Illness Facts," p. 1.
10. "What Is Bipolar Disorder?" p. 1-2, http://www.humanillness.com/Behavioral-Health-A-Br/Bipolar-Disorder.html (accessed April 12, 2008).
11. "What Are the Symptoms of Bipolar Disorder?" p. 1-2, http://www.nimh.nih.gov/health/publications/ bipolar-disorder/symptoms.shtml (accessed April 12, 2008).

[12] Ibid., 2.

[13.] "What Is Bipolar Disorder?" p. 1-2, http://www.humanillness. com/Behavioral-Health-A-Br/Bipolar-Disorder.html (accessed April 12, 2008).

[14.] WebMD Better Information. Better Health, "Bipolar Disorder Guide, Bipolar Disorder: What Is Bipolar Disorder?" reviewed by Amal Chakraburtty, on July 22, 2008, p. 1, http://www. webmd.com/bipolar-disorder/guide/what-is-bipolar-disorder.html (accessed April 14, 2008).

[15.] WebMD Better Information, Better Health, "Bipolar Disorder Guide, Bipolar Disorder: What Is Bipolar Disorder?" p. 1., reviewed by the doctors at the Cleveland Clinic Department of Psychiatry and Psychology.

[16.] David Oliver, e-mail to the author, circa 2006.

[17.] *Treatment of Bipolar Disorder: A Guide for Patients and Families* (April 2000), a postgraduate medicine special report prepared by David A. Kahn, Ruth Ross, David J. Printz, and Gary S. Sachs.

[18.] WebMD Better information, Better Health, "Causes of Bipolar Disorder: The Basics," p. 1, http://www.webmd.com/ bipolar-disorder/guide/bipolar-causes-basics.html (accessed April 19, 2008).

[19.] Ibid.

[20.] "Treatment of Bipolar Disorder: A Guide for Patients and Families," p. 1-2.

[21.] Kimberly Read and Marcia Purse, "What Causes Bipolar Disorder?" p. 2, http//www,bipolar.about.com/cs/bpbasics/a/ what_causes_bp.html (accessed October 8, 2008).

[22.] WebMD Better information, Better Health, "Preventing Bipolar Disorder,", p. 1, http://www.webmd.com/bipolar-disorder/guide/ preventing-bipolar-disorder.html (accessed April 20, 2009).

[23.] *NAMI Facts: New Treatment Options for Bipolar Disorder,* reviewed by David J. Kupfer, M.D. and Thomas Detre, professor and chair for the Department of Psychiatry and director of research at Western Psychiatric Institute and Clinic.

[24.] WebMD, "Bipolar Disorder: Bipolar Disorder and Going to Work," edited by Charlotte E. Grayson, WebMD (March 2005) p. 1, http:// www.webmdhealth.com/nl/nl.aspx?s= 270&l=%2fcontent%2fcl evelandclinic%2f106801.htm (accessed December 21, 2008).

[25.] Ibid., 1-2.

[26.] Ruben Rosario, "A bridge, a Rope, Another Family Touched by Suicide," *St. Paul Pioneer Press* (Jan. 9, 2008), 1A.

27. Kenneth Norton, MSW, LICSW, "Suicide Prevention Program Promotes Early Recognition and Treatment of Mental Illness," *NAMI Advocate* (Fall 2005) p. 9.

28. Ruben Rosario, p. 6A.

29. Rebecca Woolis, MFCC, *When Someone You Love Has a Mental Illness* (New York: G.P. Putnam's Sons, 1992), 115.

30. Citrome and Goldberg, 2005, cited in Kimberly Read, "Red Flags: Warning Signs of Suicide," p. 1, http//www,bipolar.about.com/cs/suicide/a/9805_redflags3.html (accessed April 19, 2009).

31. CDC, National Center for Injury Prevention and Control, "Suicide: Fact Sheet," http://www.cdc.gov/ncipc/factsheets/suifacts.htm (accessed February 1, 2007).

32. Ibid.

33. "Treatment of Bipolar Disorder: A Guide for Patients and Families," p. 2.

34. Judy Collins, *Sanity & Grace: A Journey of Suicide, Survival, and Strength* (New York: Penguin Group [USA] Inc., 2003), 74.

35. WebMD, "Bipolar Disorder: Suicide and Bipolar Disorder," p. 1, http://www.webmdhealth.com.html (accessed April 21, 2008).

36. Woolis, p. 119.

37. Ibid., 115, 118.

38. Ibid., 115.

39. Collins, p. 74.

40. Ibid., 79.

41. *Open Your Mind, Mental Illnesses Are Brain Disorders*, NAMI (National Institute of Mental Health), pamphlet author received in mail in 2007.

42. Woolis, *When Someone You Love*, 197-198.

43. Ibid., 20-22.

44. See www.wilder.org/research.0.html.

45. "Our Homeless: Part of a Larger Story and Community," St. Paul *Pioneer Press* (April 12, 2007), 8B.

46. Jim Randall, vice president, NAMI San Fernando Valley, "Mental Illness Is Not a Crime," *NAMI Advocate* (Fall 2006), 29.

Chapter 7

1. Everett Hale, chaplain of the U.S. Senate, 1903-1909, quoted in Lloyd John Ogilvie, *Praying through the Tough Times* (Eugene, Oregon: Harvest House Publishers, 2005), 130.

Chapter 8

[1]   Rachel Naomi Remen, *Kitchen Table Wisdom* (New York: Riverhead Books, 1996), 114.

[2]   Barbara Johnson, *Pack Up Your Gloomees in a Great Big Box, Then Sit on the Lid and Laugh!* (USA: W Publishing Group, 1993), 173.

[3]   Unfortunately my notes do not include the speaker who made these remarks or the event.

[4]   Barbara Johnson, *Pack Up Your Gloomees in a Great Big Box, Then Sit on the Lid and Laugh!* (USA: W Publishing Group, 1993), 173.

[5]   Jerry Sittser, *A Grace Disguised* (Grand Rapids, Michigan: Zondervan, 1995), 120-121.

[6]   Marilyn Willett Heavilin, *When Your Dreams Die* (Nashville, Atlanta, London, Vancouver: Thomas Nelson Publishers, 1993), 54-57.

[7]   Ibid., 60-62.

[8]   Sittser, *A Grace Disguised*, 87.

Chapter 9

[1]   Sue Abderholden, executive director, NAMI Minnesota, in a letter to friends of NAMI, June 28, 2007.

[2]   Henri J. M. Nouwen, *Out of Solitude* (Notre Dame, Indiana: Ave Maria Press, 1966), 34.

[3]   Robert R. Thompson, *Remembering: The Death of a Child* (United States of America: Sugarloaf Publishing House, 2002), 82-83.

[4]   Richard J. Obershaw, *Cry Until You Laugh* (Burnsville, Minnesota: Richard J. Obershaw, MSW, LICSW, 1992), 131.

[5]   Ibid., 146-169.

[6]   Ibid., 140-142.

[7]   Ibid., 142.

[8]   Ibid., 131-133.

[9]   Granger E. Westberg, *Good Grief* (Philadelphia: Fortress Press, 1962, 1971), 21-64.

[10] Cited in Corinne Chilstroms's book, *Andrew, You Died Too Soon* (Minneapolis: Augsburg, 1993), 82. [Source: Martin Luther, *Day by Day* (Philadelphia: Fortress Press, 1982), 204.]

[11] Westberg, *Good Grief*, 17.

[12] Ibid., 18-19.

[13] Ibid., 19.

[14] Heavilin, *When Your Dreams Die*, 20.

[15] Ibid., 21-22.

16   Westberg, *Good Grief*, 63.
17   Ibid., 64.
18   Paul V. Johnson, "Grief and Loss" presentation, Northfield Hospital, September 18, 2006.

Chapter 10

1   Remen, *Kitchen Table Wisdom*, 263-265.
2   Ibid., 265.
3   Sherwood Eliot Wirt and Kersten Beckstrom, eds., *Topical Encyclopedia of Living Quotations* (Minneapolis, Minnesota: Bethany House Publishers, 1982), 122. An asterisk follows this quote rather than an author's name, which indicates it is from the writings of coeditor Sherwood Wirt.
4   Arnaldo Pangrazzi, "Bearing the Special Grief of Suicide," *CareNotes* (St. Meinrad, Indiana: Abbey Press, 1988).
5   Harold S. Kushner, *When Bad Things Happen to Good People* (New York: Schocken Books, 1981), 15-16.
6   C. S. Lewis, *A Grief Observed* (New York: HarperCollinsPublishers, 1961, 1989) 17-18.
7   Kushner, *When Bad Things Happen*, 1-2.
8   Ibid., 21-23.
9   Philip Yancey, *Where Is God When It Hurts?* (Grand Rapids, Michigan: Zondervan, 1990), 96, 99.
10   Kushner, *When Bad Things Happen*, 85-86.
11   Ibid., 108-111.
12   Ibid., 125.
13   C. S. Lewis, *The Problem of Pain* (New York: Macmillan Publishing Company, 1973), 81.
14   Yancey, *Where Is God*, 108.
15   Ibid., 108.
16   Ibid., 82.
17   Ibid., 82-84.
18   Ibid., 82-84.
19   Ibid., 92.
20   Ibid., 146.
21   Ibid., 146-147.
22   Ibid., 109.
23   Ibid., 227-228.
24   Henri J. M. Nouwen, *Life of the Beloved* (New York: The Crossroad Publishing Company, 1992), 94.
25   Sittser, *A Grace Disguised*, 23.
26   Ibid., 10.

27   Ibid., 38-39.
28   Ibid., 32.
29   Ibid., 33-34.
30   Ibid., 35-37.
31   Robert R. Thompson, *Remembering: The Death of a Child* (United States of America: Sugarloaf Publishing House, 2002), 81-82.
32   Internet, Humorous One-liners.
33   Henri J. M. Nouwen, *Life of the Beloved* (New York: The Crossroads Publishing Company, 1992), 133.
34   Johnson, *Pack Up Your Gloomees*, 6.
35   Ibid., 64-65.
36   Ibid., 65.
37   Ibid., 65.
38   Ibid., 66.
39   Ibid., 71.
40   Ibid., 65.
41   Ibid., 15 (quoting Michael Malloy, *Christian Counseling Services Newsletter* [Spring 1992]).
42   Ibid., 15-16.

Chapter 11

1   *The United Methodist Hymnal* (Nashville, Tennessee: The United Methodist Publishing House, 1989), 707.

BIBLIOGRAPHY

When you lose someone or something you love, pain is inevitable. Books can provide comfort and helpful information. If any of these help you, I will be happy.

BOOKS

Chilstrom, Corinne. *Andrew, You Died Too Soon.* Minneapolis: Augsburg, 1993.

Collins, Judy. *Sanity & Grace: A Journey of Suicide, Survival, and Strength.* New York: Penguin Group (USA) Inc., 2003.

Haverstock, Henry W. *Henry's Hilarious One Liners.* Henry W. Haverstock, 1990. (This book was given to my son David by a friend. Excerpt on front cover read, "To one of the funniest guys I know. Thanks for all the laughs!!")

Heavilin, Marilyn Willett. *When Your Dreams Die.* Nashville, Atlanta, London, Vancouver: Thomas Nelson Publishers, 1993.

Jamison, Kay. *An Unquiet Mind.* New York City: A. A. Knopf, 1995.

Jamison, Kay. *Touched with Fire*. New York: Macmillan International, 1993.

Johnson, Barbara. *Pack Up Your Gloomees in a Great Big Box, Then Sit on the Lid and Laugh!* USA: W Publishing Group, 1993.

Kushner, Harold S. *When Bad Things Happen to Good People.* New York: Schocken Books, 1981.

Lewis, C. S. *A Grief Observed.* New York: HarperCollinsPublishers, 1961, 1989.

Lewis, C. S. *The Problem of Pain.* New York: Macmillan Publishing Co., Inc., 1973.

Luther, Martin. *Day by Day.* Philadelphia: Fortress Press, 1982.

Nouwen, Henri J. M. *Life of the Beloved.* New York: The Crossroad Publishing Company, 1992.

Nouwen, Henri J. M. *Out of Solitude.* Notre Dame, Indiana: Ave Maria Press, 1966, 1974.

Obershaw, Richard J. *Cry Until You Laugh.* Burnsville, Minnesota: Richard J. Obershaw, MSW, LICSW, 1992.

Ogilvie, Lloyd John. *Praying through the Tough Times.* Eugene, Oregon: Harvest House Publishers, 2005.

Phillips, Bob. *Phillips' Book of Great Thoughts and Funny Sayings.* Wheaton: Tyndale, 1993.

Remen, Rachel Naomi. *Kitchen Table Wisdom.* New York: Riverhead Books, 1996.

Sittser, Jerry. *A Grace Disguised.* Grand Rapids, Michigan: Zondervan, 1995.

Thompson, Robert R. *Remembering: The Death of a Child.* United States of America: Sugarloaf Publishing House, 2002.

Westberg, Granger E. *Good Grief.* Philadelphia: Fortress Press, 1962, 1971.

Wirt, Sherwood Eliot and Kersten Beckstrom, editors. *Topical Encyclopedia of Living Quotations.* Minneapolis, Minnesota: Bethany House Publishers, 1982.

Woolis, Rebecca. *When Someone You Love Has a Mental Illness.* New York: G. P. Putnam's Sons, 1992.

Wright, H. Norman. *Helping Those Who Hurt.* Minneapolis, Minnesota: Bethany House, 2003.

Yancey, Philip. *Where Is God When It Hurts?* Grand Rapids, Michigan: Zondervan, 1990.

NEWSPAPERS

Abderholden, Sue. "Sometimes the Mental Health System, Not the Parent, Is the Problem," *St. Paul Pioneer Press*, Oct. 18, 2006, 10B.

Editorial, Wilder's Homelessness Study. "Our Homeless: Part of a Larger Story and Community," *St. Paul Pioneer Press*, April 12, 2007, 8B.

Gellene, Denise, *Los Angeles Times.* "Mental Health Keeping Us Home," *St. Paul Pioneer Press*, October 7, 2007, 15A.

Gilbert, Kathy. "Quiet Crusade, Father Tries to Change Suicide Vocabulary to Save Lives," *Chattanooga Times Free Press*, April 28, 2005, E1, E4.
Rosario, Ruben. "A Bridge, a Rope, Another Family Touched by Suicide," *St. Paul Pioneer Press*, January 9, 2008, 1A, 6A.

MAGAZINES

Norton, Kenneth. "Suicide Prevention Program Promotes Early Recognition and Treatment of Mental Illness." *NAMI Advocate* (Fall 2005), 9.
Randall, Jim. "Mental Illness Is Not a Crime." *Nami Advocate* (Fall 2006), 29.

LETTERS

Letter from Darcy Taylor, director of Constituent Relations, NAMI, November 2007.
Letter from Sue Abderholden, executive director, NAMI Minnesota, friends of NAMI, June 28, 2007.

PAMPHLETS

"Addressing Mental Health: You or Someone You Love May Need Help." *Health Journal, BlueCross BlueShield BluePlus of Minnesota,* 15, no. 1 (Spring 2006): 1.
NAMI Facts: New Treatment Options for Bipolar Disorder. Reviewed by David J. Kupfer and Thomas Detre, professor and chair for the Department of Psychiatry and director of research at Western Psychiatric Institute and Clinic, received by author on February 8, 2002.
Open Your Mind, Mental Illnesses Are Brain Disorders. NAMI (National Institute of Mental Health) pamphlet author received in mail in 2007.
Pangrazzi, Arnaldo. "Bearing the Special Grief of Suicide." *CareNotes* (St. Meinrad, IN: Abbey Press, 1988).
Treatment of Bipolar Disorder: A Guide for Patients and Families. A postgraduate medicine special report, prepared by David

A. Kahn, Ruth Ross, David J. Printz, and Gary S. Sachs (April 2000).

SPEAKERS

Johnson, Paul V. "Grief and Loss" presentation, Northfield Hospital, September 18, 2006.

INTERNET

CDC National Center for Injury Prevention and Control. "Suicide: Fact Sheet." http://www.cdc.gov/nicipc/factsheets/suifacts. html (accessed February 1, 2007).

NAMI National Alliance on Mental Illness. "What is Mental Illness: Mental Illness Facts," p. 1. http://www.nami.org/ PrinterTemplate.cfm?Section=About_ Mental_Illness&Templ. html. (accessed April 26, 2008).

NIMH National Institute of Mental Health. "What Are the Symptoms of Bipolar Disorder?" p. 1. Last reviewed June 26, 2008. http://www.nimh.nih.gov/health/publications/ bipolar-disorder/symptoms.shtml (accessed April 12, 2008).

Read, Kimberly. "Red Flags: Warning Signs of Suicide," p. 1. Updated March 5, 2008. http://www.bipolar.about.com/cs/ suicide/a/9805_redflags3.html (accessed April 26, 2009).

Read, Kimberly and Marcia Purse. "What Causes Bipolar Disorder?" p. 1. http://www.bipolar.about.com/cs/bpbasics/a/ what_causes_bp.html (accessed December 11, 2008).

WebMD Better Information, Better Health. "Bipolar Disorder Guide, Bipolar Disorder: What Is Bipolar Disorder?" p. 1. Reviewed by Amal Chakraburtty on July 22, 2008. http://www. webmd.com/bipolar-disorder/guide/what-is-bipolar-disorder. html (accessed April 14, 2008).

WebMD Better information, Better Health. "Can Bipolar be Prevented?" p. 1. http://www.webmd.com/bipolar-disorder/ guide/can-bipolar-prevented.html (accessed April 16, 2008).

WebMD Better information, Better Health. "Causes of Bipolar Disorder: The Basics," p. 1. http://www.webmd.com/

bipolar-disorder/guide/bipolar-causes-basics.html (accessed
April 19, 2008).

WebMD Better information, Better Health. "Preventing Bipolar
Disorder," p.1.
http://www.webmd.com/bipolar-disorder/guide/preventing-
bipolar-disorder.html (accessed April 20, 2009).

WebMD. "Bipolar Disorder: Bipolar Disorder and Going to Work."
Edited by Charlotte E. Grayson, WebMD, March 2005. *http://
www.webmdhealth.com/nl/nl.aspx?s=270&l=%2fconten
t%2fclevelandclinic%2f106801* (accessed December 21,
2008).

WebMD. "Bipolar Disorder: Suicide and Bipolar Disorder," p. 1.
http://www.webmdhealth.com.html (accessed on April 21,
2008).

"What Is Bipolar Disorder?" p. 1. http://www.humanillness.
com/Behavioral-Health-A-Br/Bipolar-Disorder.html (accessed
April 12, 2008).

INDEX

BOOK SUMMARY

Young, handsome, and full of life, David Day is ready to marry his college sweetheart. Everything is in place: he has completed his college education and launched a successful computer career. Before he can make the most important commitment of his life, however, a thief strikes, stealing his dreams. As he wrestles with severe bipolar disease, he loses first his fiancée and then his job.

David's fighting spirit gets him through law school and helps him pass the Minnesota Bar Examination. It helps him too when the Minnesota Board of Law Examiners decides his illness makes him unfit for the challenging public law career he had chosen—a decision he courageously challenges.

His family has faith everything will come out right in the end. Surely David's hard work has earned him some good luck, some happiness. He has found a medication he can tolerate and has been hospital free for three years. As they begin to relax, bipolar strikes again, fatally this time.

In the aftermath of David's death, his mother, Pat, has to decide: Is that all there was to his life? Did the thief win? Decide for yourself as you follow Pat's compelling true-life journey. Along the way you'll learn important information about bipolar, a disease which affects 5.7 million Americans, about how to cope with mental illness when it affects you or a loved one, and about how to move forward when, in the midst of grief and loss, God seems unavailable and uncaring. You'll also discover the joy and peace available even in the darkest pit and the hope that can rise from the ashes of despair. This is a story you will find as intriguing as the movies and books you have seen and can't forget.

PATRICIA TEMPLE DAY BIO

Author Patricia Temple Day was born and raised in Northfield, Minnesota, where she graduated from St. Olaf College with a BA in business education and a minor in English. After earning an MA from the University of Minnesota, she worked fifteen years as a high school teacher and fifteen as an administrative assistant in the academic and business world. She and her husband John raised four sons on their five-generation Century Farm in Randolph, Minnesota, where they experienced for over forty years the joys and challenges that go hand in hand with bugs and weeds, volatile crop markets, constant change, and depending on the weather.

Two of Pat's anchors in the midst of turmoil have been the family farm, which has given her the opportunity to view the seasons from seed to harvest, and her church family, where she has been nurtured and has nurtured others while serving as a teacher, small group leader, and lay speaker.

Still, nothing prepared her to deal with bipolar disease, the thief that struck her family, stealing her son David's hopes and eventually his life. Whatever personal identification you give to the thief, the question is not *whether* but *when* he strikes, stealing someone or something you love. Moved by her loss, Pat wrote this book. Her goal? To help others find peace and joy in the midst of their personal storm and to find answers to the question most ask at times like these: "Where is God hiding in the midst of my pain?"

AFTERWORD

Bipolar disorder is a psychiatric illness that epidemiologists report to be present in 1 percent of the population. Studies over recent years have shown that it is a serious disorder which not only can be excruciatingly painful for the person suffering from the disease but can markedly interfere with interpersonal relationships, work, and family life. It also has been well documented that people with bipolar disorder are at substantial risk of ending their own lives. Thus, the goal of Pat Day to describe her experiences with her son's battle with bipolar disorder brings to life an amazing story which can benefit readers of all walks of life.

As a professor of psychiatry at the University of Minnesota, I would note that this book can be of special usefulness to medical students and residents in understanding the personal side of severe psychiatric illness. Further, her discussion of the functions of NAMI is useful and can also be helpful to others.

Pat Day's book is startlingly candid in its description of her son's life and of the life of her family. Following a tragedy, it would be understandable that many people would withdraw from examining or describing their experiences. Pat Day's ability to share her experiences is amazingly generous and is most touching.

Beyond the aspect of the book which clearly describes personal issues and also describes very informative aspects of bipolar disorder are the classical quotations that put her experiences in a universal context.

In summary, Pat Day has provided a remarkable gift which I hope many people will take advantage of.

S. Charles Schulz, MD
Donald W. Hastings Endowed Chair
Professor and Head, Department of Psychiatry
University of Minnesota Medical School

Edwards Brothers,Inc!
Thorofare, NJ 08086
19 May, 2010
BA2010139